# Childcare Revealed

## A guide through the ups & downs of a challenging profession

# Childcare Revealed

## A guide through the ups & downs of a challenging profession

## Peggy Steward

Jamison Street Preschool
Pensacola, Florida

Jamison Street Preschool
Pensacola, Florida
www.jamisonstreetpreschool.com

# ﻌﺍ Table of Contents ﻌﺍ

# INTRODUCTION

My friends have said, "You could write a book about your adventures in childcare!" I have always thought it would be a good idea as many people do not understand what childcare personnel actually do. They do not understand that our great love for children gets us through the long hours and the smelly diapers. Childcare is a very tough, demanding job with low wages, but I can't imagine doing anything more rewarding with my life.

As a small child, my life was a series of ups and downs. My father was in the Merchant Marines and was out to sea when my mother left. She left my sister and me at eighteen months old in a basket in the yard outside our home. My father came home that day and found us soiled and teary-eyed with no furniture in the house.

He was devastated and did what he could at the time for us. This meant numerous foster homes and orphanages (until I was about seven years old) as a custody fight began between the grandparents. I only remember that I was not the "wanted one" because I looked too much like our mother. What a reason to dislike a child—why not because she was dirty, skinny, stupid, or that she was out-spoken and didn't like to have her hair washed? But no—she resembled a mother who for her own reasons left her husband and two small children. So let's not want her oldest daughter!

Eventually my father married my stepmother. In later years, I admired this woman. She took in two children who were not her own, who could not brush their teeth, etc. She had an eleven-month-old child of her own. Over the years, she told us, "You are not my children," and "I can send you away." These comments may not sound too harsh, but to a small child growing up without being in the family pictures, it lowered my sister's and my self-esteem.

We were not able to form friendships as our father was transferred often. But we did have compassionate teachers. I remember one year in high school, my teacher gave me a box of pre-owned clothes. What special feelings I had! My clothing up until that time was purchased several sizes too large so I could "grow into them." With the gift of the pre-owned clothes, I had clothes that fit properly.

As I became a young woman, who didn't date much, all I could think of was having children of my own. I wanted a houseful. I felt like a queen when my husband and I married. My husband, Joe, is such a warm and caring man. We immediately started working on the "houseful" of children. I worked at an insurance company until I was six months pregnant and then stayed home and knitted clothes for my baby. We purchased a pre-owned crib and painted everything on it—the springs, screws and railings too. Now the room was ready for our child. I was driven by one goal—to be a better mother than mine.

What joy came to us with our daughter Michelle! Michelle was the "perfect" baby to start our family with. I had read numerous books on caring for a baby, and I soon became a good mother. Our daughter taught me that I could sleep all night—the books said that I would be up often. Wow, this was way too easy being a mother! My husband and I felt so warm and excited to share her with others. We thought she was the most precious child around and of course so very smart. We decided that she needed a sibling.

When our own Michael arrived how thrilled we were, even Michelle thought that we had him for her only. Mike was a little different than Michelle. He was up all night as he developed colic during his first three months. Now my parenting skills were challenged. He cried a lot and I did not know what to do. I wanted to make him more comfortable, care for our daughter and home, but how? I wondered if I had done something wrong during my pregnancy, and if I had somehow harmed my baby. These things I grew to understand were not my fault, but the feelings were there anyway.

I learned through trial and error that wrapping Mike up in a blanket (swaddling-style) eased his discomfort. How I wished that I knew someone who had been through this situation and could give me some advice.

2

Now that my parenting skills were challenged, I needed a new strategy to keep harmony in our lives. My husband and I decided that I would be a stay-at-home mom. I was the primary caregiver. This was great with me, as I only wanted to be with my babies. The children brought so much love and joy into our lives. I wanted to spend more time with them in lieu of housework so we cleaned the house together, they brought along their toys from room to room with me. Michelle pushed Mike around in his stroller when he was fussy in the room, sometimes singing to him. We would go outside daily for picnics, baseball, basketball, and wagon rides. When they took a nap so did I—I wanted to have the same energy that they did!

In later years I thought if we all cleaned together, then we could go to the park sooner. This would be good practice as they became older. So they began to help make their beds, pick up their toys, and help feed the dog, even if that meant just walking behind me as helpers. Then we would make sandwiches and go off to our adventure of the day. Sometimes it was just in the backyard.

As the children became older we did Cub Scouts, Girl Scouts, baseball, football, soccer, band and drama. The numerous school plays we attended and the sports games were all times to be remembered. One year both children played soccer. At the end of the season, a game was played between the parents and children. Michelle and Mike were on different teams due to their ages. After playing against the children for two games back to back, I had a new respect for soccer players.

I enjoyed watching our children grow. Their motor skills developed along with their cognitive skills. How rewarding it was to see them struggle with a math subject and then finally achieve it. Our motto "you can do anything you want to if you try and think positive" always won out.

When our children became young adults in high school, I felt a need to do something out of the home. Friends had told me about the "empty-nest syndrome" and it wasn't something I wanted. As my children turned out terrific, I felt that I had a lot to give other children. Today's parents are often not as fortunate as I was to be able to stay at home, so I thought maybe I could help a child to be loved and productive out of their parents' arms, or to help ease a parent's frustration of having to leave their child at a childcare center.

I had raised two children and managed our home, so I thought that working in a childcare center should be easy. I soon found out that the time I spent with children was very rewarding but also very challenging. The children were like little sponges with such a thirst and desire to learn.

I soon found myself caught up in classes that were mandatory for me to take to continue to work in childcare. To work as more than a substitute teacher, a lot of things needed to be done by me and all cost me money (see Chapter 2). Over the years, I took classes and workshops from various agencies and joined a professional organization to help me to become a better teacher for these young children.

I have learned a lot about children, how they think, how their brains develop and, of course, "secrets" to Toilet Independence. On many occasions, I have wished that I had this knowledge to use with my children when they were growing up. Childcare centers then were not available everywhere and the cost was very high.

The longer I stay in the childcare field, the more I know how important the teachers are. How we help a child to socialize with others and prepare them for kindergarten are things much needed. Our daughter cried the first month of school whenever her teacher gave her a paper to do. We had played school at home and did "school work," but not AT SCHOOL. How she would have had that anxiety reduced or removed had she went to a quality childcare setting before starting school! (See Chapter 1.)

Today's parents have a tough time. Many family units are an adult and a child while many grandparents are still working, and not retired to be able to help with the children. Who is there for the parents while they are struggling to make ends meet financially? Where do they get help with their child's problems? Our neighbors are busy doing the same thing and many of us do not even know their names. Where do young parents get help from, if not from their child's teachers?

I had a friend who found a nanny to help her with her daily life. My friend had two children—an infant and a child of eight years old. She had a great job with retirement benefits and a good medical package. She did not wish to quit her job to stay home with her infant. A nanny was just what her family needed. The nanny came every morning, helped the older child off to school, bathed the baby, and cared for the infant's needs. The nanny did the laundry, cleaned the house, helped make cookies for the son's Cub Scout meetings and sometimes started supper for the evening. She was an asset to this young mother. When my friend came home each day, the chores that fill others' lives were done and she could spend her time with the children. Unfortunately, this is not an option for all families.

I feel strongly that our jobs as childcare teachers is to first provide for the safety of all children, and second to assist all parents in their endeavors to be the best parents they can be. The child's parents are his/her first teachers and know the child best, but the parents do need advice from time to time. This is where we come in.

I remember when I first obtained my CDA (see Chapter 2), someone approached me on the phone from the local paper, asking about childcare and the new CDA requirements mandated by the state. Of all my positive comments about this profession, the writer chose to end his article with my comment, "A garbage collector makes more money than a childcare worker." I wasn't flattered by this article and was not sure if the garbage collector would ever take my trash again, but the message is still the same today. Childcare providers are critical for families. That is why we need more caring people to join our profession.

When parents have a problem with their child or something isn't going right at home, they usually will voice it, or you can tell from their mood or action that something is troubling them. It is our job as teachers to assist them. When parents keep their child home with them on their day off but express how tired they are, it is our opportunity to remind them that the childcare center is open, why not bring the child to school and have a fun day to themselves or do the cleaning or shopping and then come pick their child up early. (See Chapter 7, for a good example.) What a difference staff at a childcare center can make!

Over my twenty years working in the childcare industry, I have had the opportunity to give classes to parents and other childcare workers. One that is always full is the Positive Discipline class. Parents are seeking ways to enforce positive behavior without spanking. "How is this accomplished?" "The children push me to my limits." "Time-out doesn't work." "I am tired of being the mean guy." "What can I do, I work all day and then have to listen to their crying?" These are all questions and comments that I have heard. Some parents have even called me at home seeking help.

As a professional, I need to know the answers to these questions to assist parents with their problems. If I don't have an answer or am unsure, I will always find someone in the community who can or I will refer them to a good book on the subject. I do not have all the answers but I do know things that work over a period of time. Parents grow to trust the advice their child's teacher gives to them.

A Human Development across the Lifespan course that I took once has given me much food for thought. We covered topics such as genetics, adoption, and how traits are transmitted, theories of development, the importance of good nutrition and play, moral development and influence of peers. The knowledge of how important my job is became quite clear. With constant training in my field, I can become an important member of society through helping form young children into productive adults along with the help of their parents. Some of my classmates questioned the purpose of pushing young children into a preschool setting. Of course, I couldn't keep my mouth shut on this subject! I explained that childcare can help provide the socialization that is needed to function in today's society, and that children must learn to share, to come to terms with whatever obstacles were thrown their way, even at a young age. I went on to remind them that childcare centers are not rigid settings. We have warm, caring adults who give children a positive learning atmosphere. All mothers were not meant to be "stay at home mothers." Some parents function better when their child goes to preschool and they are able to give quality care when they come home from work. I also reminded them that birth through three years are the years that children developed the most; why not take advantage of that? Do you know that at this young age, a child can learn a foreign language better than at an older age?

As professionals in the childcare field we have so much knowledge to share with the general community. We do assist parents and children under our care to be the best that they can be. We are not babysitters nor do we expect young children to be in an inflexible classroom with lessons all day. They need plenty of hands-on activities.

It is amazing that at every workshop I hold, the question always asked is, "How do I get my children to bed at night and to sleep in their own bed, not in mine?" The first parent to ask this question is always sided with numerous other parents. They always are relieved to know that they are not the only ones with this problem. So by having workshops for parents, hosted by their child's teachers from the childcare center, parents feel less guilty about what they are doing and learn that so many others are going through the same things. Other fears and anxieties come out and the parents share their solutions or advice with each other. It is great to sit back and watch them interact with each other, to exchange phone numbers for play time for the children and even shared babysitting times. What more could I ask for than for the parents of the children under my care to feel less threatened by feeling that they don't have the skills that they need, and to develop a better feeling of "I'M OKAY TODAY!"

In addition to providing parents with a different perspective on childcare, this book will be beneficial to anyone interested in working in a childcare setting. You will learn what goes on day-to-day, as well as the rules and regulations that guide a center in its quest to provide a strong environment for the little ones that are our future. You will be offered a glimpse into the ways teachers and administrators go through each day and see what they need to do to keep a center up and running. There are examples of how teachers and parents can work together to best meet the needs of a child.

I wrote this book in the hopes that anyone who reads it realizes that we (teachers, assistants and caregivers) are indeed an important part of a young child's life. Our job is to provide a learning environment, not babysitting services.

I hope you will find my experiences interesting and that you learn a little something about this rewarding profession that enables young minds to grow as it puts them on the path to their future.


Peggy

# ‿ﻞ Chapter 1 ﻟﻌ
## Childcare

This first chapter is an important one for parents and for childcare professionals who help parents to make choices. I will provide insights into the nature of childcare, so parents can make informed decisions about the type of quality care desired for a child.

Some of the things that parents need to consider are a childcare center's goals and philosophy. Do these coincide with their views? License information is also important. Does a center's child-to-staff ratio meet the state's rules? What is the health department's view of the cleanliness of the center? What is the staff turnover rate? Parents can only know this by visiting various childcare centers to see for themselves if a center meets the standards that they want for their child.

What about contacting the local Children's Services Center? One can check licensing, inspections and complaint history by contacting the Department of Children and Families licensing center. In Florida, the website www.myflorida.com/childcare allows anyone to check on inspection reports.

As the first three years of life are so important for development, the learning environment plays a key role in a child's future. But what type of learning does each parent wish for his/her child? As you will see in this chapter, a parent must consider many options before entering their child into a childcare setting.

Parents need to search out and visit a childcare center prior to placing their child there. They need to meet the director and the staff who will be working with their child. When parents have selected the center, they will want to stay in touch with the staff. Sometimes a problem arises; the parent knows the child better than anyone else does, and may have some solutions to the problem. Good communication can only benefit the child.

It is also the responsibility of a childcare worker to keep in touch with the parents. The parents are in fact paying the childcare employees' salaries and made their choice of childcare based at least partially on a good reputation. Maintaining a good relationship with parents will keep that reputation secure and encourage others to choose the childcare center.

## WHAT IS CHILDCARE?

To me childcare is care given to all children of all ages in a safe learning environment. Many family units (single parents, grandparents, or husband-wife teams, etc.) feel that their children will be best prepared for kindergarten by placement in quality care outside of the home. A childcare center is a safe place for a child to go and to learn valuable skills to become ready for kindergarten and beyond.

A typical center is open from 6 a.m. to 6 p.m. Monday through Friday. A center is usually divided into classrooms according to children's ages. Each room will have age-appropriate furniture, toys, and books available for children to use. Each classroom will have the appropriate number of adults, based on the state staff-to-child ratio, who are trained as early childhood professionals.

The children in each room will have opportunities to explore, to make friends, and to develop language and motor skills. They will have daily lessons on subjects of interest for their age, often singing songs to boost language skills. There will be many activities to develop eye-hand coordination and cognitive skills. The children will eat breakfast, lunch and a snack at the center. Because they are young children, they will also have one or two naps throughout the day.

A major factor for parents is the location of the childcare center. They will usually want a center that is on the way to work and home. If a child should become sick during the day, it is important to most parents that they can quickly come pick-up their child.

Another factor parents look for is the cost of tuition. It is difficult to say whether the cost outweighs other factors or not. Often, a parent must forego the first choice and opt for something more affordable.

## TYPES OF CENTERS

There are many types of childcare centers available for parents to consider. The center where I first worked was church-based, as are many in our area. Interestingly, the families who brought their children to the center had different religious beliefs and selected the center for various reasons such as quality of care, price and location.

Some centers are franchises, with the same name and program in other states. There are many for-profit centers, while others remain non-profit. There are also some centers that are offered on-site at public schools.

Many childcare centers accept children from newborn through age 12 (for before and after school care). Most centers accept school-age children before and after school, including on school holidays, for the convenience of parents who may have other children at the center or are looking for additional childcare.

## CURRICULUM

The curriculum in a childcare center is the teaching style and methods used for daily lesson plans. There are many types of curriculum to choose from. Each childcare center has its own philosophy and a specific curriculum that fits into their program.

One school environment with its own specific approach to educational needs is a Montessori school. This program is focused on the child being an active participant with the teacher being less directly involved. The Montessori approach is self-directed and has mixed-age groups. The children learn at their own pace by using real objects, not toy ones. This approach helps the children to understand their world by discovery of materials available. The children learn at their own pace, with self-directed activities and teacher observations throughout the day. Children are often accepted from birth thru middle-school age.

Another type of program is High Reach, which provides a nine-month curriculum to help teachers teach the basics. Each month they provide a Teacher's Guide, a developmental skills checklist, parent newsletters, along with items for promoting that month's theme. The cost for this varies according to the number of children within the classroom. The curriculum is available for ages three months to kindergarten. High Reach also provides training workshops for staff and other learning materials.

Early Start is a preschool curriculum for age two to five. This program provides teachers with daily lesson plans, activity sheets for each child, and it can be used in large or small learning centers. Early Start costs are based on the number of children within an age group.

Wee Learn is available for infants through preschool and is a faith-based curriculum. The curriculum guides daily activities with a Bible story and verses for each unit or theme.

High Scope has a curriculum for infants through adolescents. It offers opportunities for children to learn by becoming actively involved with their daily routine. These children have small and large group activities and go through a process of planning what they want to do, how to do it, and then tell their teacher what they have done.

The Creative Curriculum is one that I found to work for various teaching styles. As a hands-on teacher, this curriculum leaves me with flexibility to provide work materials for the children to explore. This program is very informative as to what the teacher's role and the family's role are, and offers materials for all developmental areas.   The Creative Curriculum also has an assessment tool kit to help with the assessment of children. Their website www.teachingstrategies.com provides a site to help create strategies to assist the children to reach their developmental skill level. It's a great tool for classroom teachers to gain knowledge as to the developmental level of each child and for the director and parents to know that the children are learning at their level or above. When a child is behind or needs extra help in an area, the teacher can print out assorted ways for the parents to assist their child at home.   This is a great way for parents and teachers to work together in the common interest of the child.

I am familiar with these curricula through taking workshops and visiting other centers. There are more curricula available than the ones mentioned here. Many books are available through catalogs such as Hammetts, ABC, and your local stores. (See Index.) I use a variety of resources for my daily lessons. Some of my favorite books from which to obtain information are:

1. Active Learning Series
2. Wee Care
3. The Instant Curriculum for Busy Teachers of Young Children
4. Totline Theme-a-saurus
5. The Mailbox Magazine

The Index provides addresses for these books as well as others that I use frequently.

To me, quality care is most important. In a childcare center, children are exposed to others from all walks of life. They can be shown at an early age how important it is to treat others with respect. The young children in our care are full of energy, eager and ready to meet new challenges. To best harness these attributes and give a child the opportunity to thrive, a childcare center must provide the best possible teachers with lots of resources.

I strongly feel after over two decades of experience with childcare that I have seen childcare grow in purpose and in size. As the need for quality childcare grows, many more professionals who are dedicated are needed to fill the void.

As you have seen in this chapter, parents must consider several options before entering their child in a center. A person who is interested in working in a childcare center faces similar choices. You will want to find a childcare center that fits your views too. It is nice when the two coincide. I wish you good luck in finding the center that is right for you.

# ᴖ Chapter 2 ᴖ
## Staffing

This chapter is the heart and soul of any childcare center. The director and teachers are so important. Do they know the philosophy of the center and follow its guidelines? Are they equipped with the knowledge of how children function in addition to all of the other information a childcare worker should know? These things are so important to both the parent and to the adult interested in working in childcare.

Some people in our society view childcare personnel as merely babysitters. After reading this chapter, I am sure that you will agree with me that this is far from true. As you will learn, a profession in childcare is an extremely hard one with few benefits and enormous responsibility.

What does a director of a childcare center do? Does she or he sit at a desk all day or play with the children? What work is involved to keep a center open and functioning?

I will answer these questions in this chapter. In this chapter, we will discuss the importance of staffing in a childcare center. What are the various positions available? What role is played by each and what training is needed? We will discuss the benefits involved and several organizations that are available to assist teachers.

In order to have the most qualified teachers, we must search for them. Over the last two decades I have seen many teachers come and go. We have had the good fortune to hire some wonderful teachers who really enjoy educating young ones to the best of their abilities. Unfortunately, we have also hired staff members who only looked upon childcare centers as babysitting companies–this is far from true. Some employees have thought they could just sit around all day, commanding children to do this or that. One employee thought that screaming across the playground for a child to stop throwing sand was an effective way to handle the situation. It did not even cross her mind to go to the child to talk about his misbehavior or to re-direct him to another area. We have also had staff members work with us who would not clean up a room, take trash out or clean a toilet. At one time, we hired a female who was a stripper at night. What a surprise we had when a male parent asked us, "Why is _____ working with my child? She strips at a local club downtown." I don't know who we were more surprised at—ourselves for not knowing (her fingerprint and background check, and her references never showed this side of her) or the father for admitting that he frequented strip clubs.

Staffing is not an easy thing to do at a childcare center. The first thing a center must do is to set the hours of operation, decide the age of the children to attend, and choose the curriculum to be followed. After this is accomplished, it is time for the interview and hiring process. Each childcare center has its own views on the qualifications they would like their staff to have. However, all centers agree that in order to meet the obligations to the parents of the children under their care and to meet state licensing requirements, staff members must be chosen very carefully.

To provide a high-quality learning environment to all children, a center must hire people who are knowledgeable about how a child develops. Those in charge must recognize the attributes that a person must have to become a team member of their childcare center. Most childcare centers have a lead teacher in each classroom, with an assistant and an afternoon caregiver. At the center where I work, we look for our teachers to have a strong knowledge of children and to help train or guide their assistants and caregivers to obtain more education too.

The children under our care look to their teacher to give guidance in playing with others, for support when they are afraid, to keep them safe, and to ease their discomforts with lots of smiles and hugs. Teachers need to get down on the children's level, rather than hovering over them. We have to be prepared to let them know that we understand that they want their Mommy and Daddy, and be able to explain that they are at school or work and will return as soon as they can. When a child misbehaves, the child wants us to show the way, to help find words to express the needs and wants in the place of hitting, biting, and screaming.

A lead teacher's job is more demanding than that of her assistant or caregiver, but <u>every position is equally important</u>. Any adult who works with young children needs to know that no matter what job title is held, the children are the most important part of the job. They need to be familiar with the developmental stages of children and to learn how to re-direct their misbehavior. A trip to time-out, a trip to the office or a note home to the parent/guardian is only a quick fix. Drawing attention away from the bad behavior can prevent it from gaining credence, perhaps inhibiting it from becoming an established behavior.

Parents pay our salaries, so they should expect their child to get the best they can while in our care. This is why all staff members need to remember that whenever you are in a child's presence, you must act like a professional. As we all know, childcare is not a highly-paid profession. Working in childcare allows a person the opportunity to find inner fulfillment in helping small children learn and grow. As with any job, longevity and dedication can lead to increased wages and benefits.

One of the ways to become a professional is to take the Child Development Associate (CDA) course outlined below.

<u>WHAT IS A CDA?</u>

*Q. Is it required for all childcare personnel? What benefits does it give to someone? Should it be obtained prior to working in a center?*

There are two types of CDAs—one is a state equivalency and the other is a national CDA. The Council for Professional Recognition grants the National CDA, or the Child Development Associate Credential. Across states, the requirements vary.

In order to apply for the National CDA, a person must be eighteen years old, must have a high school diploma or a GED and have worked with children for about 480 hours.

http://www.cdacouncil.org/cda_obt.htm

You must first order a packet, sending a check for $18.00 plus shipping and handling. After filling this out, you can then start the process to obtain your CDA. This usually takes about 1½ to 2 years to complete before you receive your certificate.

A National CDA has six competency goals:

Goal 1 -- to maintain a safe, healthy learning environment.
Goal 2 -- to advance the physical and intellectual competence.
Goal 3 -- to support social and emotional development; to provide guidance.
Goal 4 -- to establish positive and productive relationships with families.
Goal 5 -- to ensure a well-run, purposeful program responsive to participant needs.
Goal 6 -- to maintain a commitment to professionalism.

(http://www.cdacouncil.org/cda_obt.htm)

During my CDA class at our local college, we were responsible for setting-up files for each goal, including sub-files to keep all our information detailing how we were going to implement these goals within our classrooms.

In addition to the coursework, a professional visits the classroom for several hours of classroom observation. The observer watches you interact with the children, takes notes, but does not communicate with you during the observation or after. You must also send out questionnaires to the parents of the children within your care, and have them returned to you in sealed envelopes. These you mail to the Council in Washington, D.C., along with the classroom observation documents, your college credit class and grade, a filing fee, your documented first aid class, and proof that you belong to an Early Childhood organization. It usually takes several months for this information to be evaluated and for your certificate to be mailed to you. The first certificate is good for three years. Then you must send off for a renewal packet. In order to renew, the work is similar.

This process is very worthwhile, as you will obtain a lot of useful information to help today's parents. You will also be in a class of your peers, which can help you gain knowledge, insight, and even friendship.

The address for the Council is below:

Council for Professional Recognition
2460 16<sup>th</sup> Street, NW
Washington, DC 20009-3575
202-265-9090 or 800-424-4310
http://www.cdacouncil.org/

## SALARIES

Although there are not many traditional employee benefits as a childcare provider and the salary is low, most centers do have something worthwhile to offer an employee.

Some of the salaries for personnel in a childcare center start at minimum wage. The wages go up according to the degree of training. A staff member who has a college degree or a CDA will earn a greater salary. The staff member who has a degree and CDA plus years of experience in a childcare center will start out with an even higher salary.

As we learned in Chapter 1, there are many different types of childcare centers. Franchised centers will often offer higher starting salaries than privately-owned and non-profit centers. A larger center will usually pay salaries higher than a smaller one. Please remember that there is only so much money coming in each week from the children's tuition/fees and all the expenses of a childcare center must be met to keep the doors open. Eighty-five percent or more of all expenses of a center may be for salaries.

## BENEFITS

Some large centers participate in an insurance program for workers, but most childcare centers do not offer health insurance for employees. Most centers do offer vacation time and paid personal days. As with most jobs, paid days off usually increase the longer you stay at the same establishment. Something to remember is that when you are not at work, a substitute must be arranged to replace you that day and paid as well.

The employee who is trustworthy and remains at one center will reap more benefits than the worker who goes from one center to another for short periods. Frequent teacher changes are often upsetting to the children as well. Stability and routine usually make it easier when a child is apart from his/her parent(s).

My <u>most</u> important benefits are the daily hugs and smiles that I get from the children. Working with a two-year-old as he struggles with Toilet Independence can be strenuous (for child, staff, and parent), but when that child has successfully pulled down and up their own pants and tells you with a great big smile, "I did it by myself!" –well let me tell you that it is benefit enough for me.

If you are looking for paid benefits, a high salary and a lot of time off, then childcare is not for you. However, if you would like to jump in with both feet, catch whatever cold is going around that day and make a child feel that you care, then please apply at a local center for employment. You won't regret it!

<u>ORGANIZATIONS</u>

As teachers of young children, we must seek the help of our peers from time to time. One way to do this is to join early childhood organizations. There are many available to join, and I have listed a few in the Index.

One organization that I have belonged to for many years is the National Association for the Education of Young Children (NAEYC). We have a local branch in Pensacola and that is one reason I chose it over the numerous others. The local board plans workshops and brings in well-known speakers throughout the year. There are conferences, where vendors come from all over to show and to sell their educational materials. This is much better than shopping through catalogs! Some of the speakers that we have had were Bev Box, Jean Feldman, and Mimi Chenfeld.

By becoming a member of NAEYC or any other early childhood organization, you have a wide variety of people to turn to for the latest information on children and to assist you in your classrooms. In return, you must be an active participant too, whether you have the time to attend all meetings or not. Part of our job should involve being accessible to others who want to join the field, showing them the way, taking them under our wing and leading them to become the best they can be. It is very disappointing when people do not want to share their knowledge and aid others as they start on the path of childcare. The childcare field is extremely demanding, with long hours, low wages and few benefits. Becoming a part of the childcare community brings a stronger sense of purpose in addition to supplying knowledge and aid to help one grow as a teacher.

I have listed several organizations in the Index. I am sure there are many more, but these should give you a beginning point. I suggest that you send for information from several of the organizations to see which will fill your needs. Learning everything possible about better ways to help children will make your job even more rewarding.

DIRECTOR

To give a high quality-learning environment for all children, a center must hire personnel who are knowledgeable in the details of child development. It is vitally important that the director or owner have this knowledge also. In order to find the best staff available, she or he must be able to recognize all the attributes that a person needs to become a team member of the childcare center.

A Director in the State of Florida now must have a credential called the "Florida Child Care and Education Program Administrator Credential." This is given on two levels. Level 1 is the Foundational Level and Level 2 is an Advanced Level. To maintain this credential, it must be renewed every five years.

The educational requirements for the Foundational Level are:

1. High School diploma or GED.

2. The Department of Children and Families mandated Part 1 introductory childcare course.
3. The ten-hour module Developmentally Appropriate Practices for Children with Special Needs or an 8-hour in-service training course in serving children with disabilities.
4. One of the following: a Child Development Associate credential (CDA); an approved Florida CDA Equivalency; a formal education exemption qualification (including a waiver); or a documented employment history recognition exemption.
5. One course in the curriculum content area Overview of Childcare Center Management.

The educational requirements are one year of experience in on-site childcare and education program administration.

The educational requirements for the Advanced Level are the same as Foundational Level plus two additional approved courses in childcare education and program administration, or an exemption.

The educational requirements are two years of experience in on-site childcare and education program administration.

The above information was taken from the Administrator's Credential packet available by writing to the following:

Administrator Credential Coordinator
Florida Children's Forum
2807 Remington Green Circle
Tallahassee, FL 32308
1-877-FLTEACH (358-3224)

The course that I took in Management to meet my requirements for the credential was very informative. As this was a college class, I went three hours one night a week for a semester. I was in a classroom with several of my peers who I had met at other workshops. Some were already directors/owners and were getting their credential as well. The State of Florida has recently made it mandatory that all director/owners have this credential.

There are many directors of childcare centers who lack the knowledge of what it takes to be one. A director may be hired because she/he has a degree. This degree may not be in Early Childhood Education and a course like this one will help them. This class leaves no doubt as to the amount of paperwork, time and energy spent during the day and at home on weekends to be a director.

Each employee looks to the director for solutions to her/his problems—within the classroom, in dealing with parents, and even with personal problems. A director must have the knowledge to help a staff member who is seeking advice. The director needs to have the answers for the staff or at least know where to find the answers. To maintain a good working relationship, the director must be available to help with each staff member's problem. Sometimes the problem is minor, but sometimes it requires seeking out a solution. These problems vary from a parent who forgets the child's lunch several times a week, a child's misbehavior in the classroom, needing a new idea for a parent gift at Christmas, or just listening to someone vent that this year's class is a challenging one.

A director must have a list of substitutes handy in addition to the ability to re-arrange staff to meet the State child-to-staff ratios when someone is not able to come to work. Having team players who are willing to help is essential too. Sometimes, the director must work a classroom. It is not a bad idea for the director to work a classroom anyway. By being involved in the classroom setting, a director can see what the staff member of that classroom goes through each day. This could be beneficial to everyone.

Because staffing is the most costly item in childcare, a director needs to spend lots of time with her or his staff. The director should visit each classroom at different times of the day, visit the playground and even the lunchroom. All responsibility comes down to the director if there is an issue between staff members, parent and staff, or child and staff. A director needs to see this potential problem and care for it immediately, not wait for another person to confront her with it. In other words, she needs to have eyes in the back of her head and be everywhere at one time.

There are many additional duties for the busy director. A director needs to know how a center operates, including how to manage expenses. Timely payments of bills and salaries are important. The endless paperwork, budgets to prepare, and the tracking of tuition are just a few other challenges.

There are several ways to keep records at a childcare center. Some people use computer software and some continue to use paper logs. Either way, the director has much paperwork to attend to daily.

Some directors have the advantage of an assistant. After many years as a teacher, I was given the added responsibility of assistant to the director. I often helped the director carry-out some of the tasks that she sometimes could not complete in a day. By having an assistant, the director can shift some of her responsibilities so she can concentrate on other things. Moreover, when the director is away from the center, it is helpful to have someone there who can assist parents or staff with any problem that may arise.

The job of staffing is so very important for a childcare center. The director must always have staff to cover all classrooms and always be on the lookout for new staff. The turnover in childcare personnel is hard on the parents, the children and the center overall. A center does not want to be caught short-handed.

We need to educate young people and old too on the importance of having staff who care about children's welfare and learning. These children are our future, so preparing them properly is a necessity. If you are not working at a childcare center now but have some extra time—volunteer at one. Let children know that someone cares.

# ⨾ Chapter 3 ⨽
## Operation of a Childcare Center

The operation of a childcare center has many different aspects. One of the director's duties is the scheduling of all teachers, caregivers, assistants, and maintenance personnel. Due to its importance, I covered staffing in the last chapter. Rules and regulations are also extremely important to the operation of a childcare center. Every state has a different set of guidelines. This chapter will cover our state's rules and regulations as an example. The Cost of Operation section in this chapter will cover the items that are a necessary part of the day-to-day expenses. I will also discuss the illnesses that children often have and ways to keep that to a minimum with strict methods of cleaning the center. Your childcare center would not be able to keep their doors open without following the policies of the state in which it is located.

Please enjoy this chapter, as it is of vital importance to all centers.

RULES AND REGULATIONS

Our state has a mandatory course consisting of forty hours of rules and regulations. This course will help individuals to become acquainted with things such as staff-to-child ratio, the proper height of fences, the space needed for each child in a classroom, the proper method of hand-washing, childhood illnesses, and the observation of children. Each person who wishes to work in a childcare center MUST have this course within ninety days of employment. This course will help staff know the required knowledge to keep children safe.

Another rule that is required by my state is that one staff member must be on the premises at all times who has taken a CPR and a First Aid course. Can you imagine not having these wonderful courses? What if a child jumped out of a swing and hurt an arm or leg? Would you know how to check for discoloration or swelling or how to immobilize the limb until the child's parent arrived? What would you do about the child who fell off a bench at the table and hit his head? Would you be able to check the size of the child's pupils, keep the child still, and know to call for an ambulance in case of a head injury or concussion? What about the child who had a seizure? What would you do?

These are all things that could happen and have happened over the years that I have worked in childcare. I was extremely glad to know that I could help the child until a trained professional from the health field could arrive. These are situations you hope never to encounter but when you are involved with children anything can happen. They are so full of energy and their listening ears are sometimes busy with other things and they didn't hear you say "sit on your bottom when at the table."

By requiring these courses, we know that the children under our care are going to get the most out of our center, and that is SAFETY. This course is also needed to help other staff. Over the years, I have called an ambulance twice for staff members who have passed out or were incoherent because of illness. We keep on file staff emergency numbers and the name of any medication they currently take. In this regard we can assist the paramedics with evaluation of our staff too.

The observation course that is included in the state mandated classes is extremely useful. Our job as teachers, assistants, or caregivers is to be the best we can be for the young children under our care. We see children as young as six weeks old now in childcare, and sometimes during the week we are with the child more than the parent/guardian. This is no fault of the parents, it is just the way today's society works. While the children are under our care, we can check on the progression of their physical growth, the state of their vision, and their language development, noting any specific challenges. We also can see and note any misbehavior that is not age-appropriate or "normal" for children.

Our coursework provides us with developmental checklists and areas that we can easily recognize as possible problems. The duty of a trained childcare professional is to log the things that we see happening and to report our findings to the director/owner. At that time the director will discuss the matter with the child's parent/guardian. The parent may consult the child's physician, etc. but we DO NOT MAKE ANY DIAGNOSIS of what we may or may not suspect—remember, we are trained childcare professionals, but we are not nurses, doctors, psychologists, etc. We only observe the children and consult with our superiors. Nothing is worse than a teacher telling a child's parents that their child has a learning problem (mislabeling the child) when that is not the case. The truth might be that the teacher has a classroom of noisy boys, and screaming girls, with no assistant and she is up to her eyeballs in paperwork. Sometimes we as teachers get bogged down in "stuff" and forget when we should be seeking other methods of helping a bright, spirited child to quiet down during certain times of the day.

The memory below of children playing outside is one of my favorites because it reminds me that not all people are cut-out for childcare.

One summer a new employee did not want to go outside. She said it was too hot for her. I realize that we live in the state of Florida and it is hot, but it is not Arizona, which is VERY HOT. I explained to her that our class of two-year-olds goes out daily even if just for fifteen minutes. The children need to use their large motor skills by running, jumping, throwing and kicking balls. They need to fill, dump and make "cakes" in the sandbox. I also explained that swinging, sliding, climbing, and riding bikes were all things the children needed to develop all their muscles. Additionally, the exercise will help the children stay fit and healthy and they will be ready for a nap later in the day. Naturally, we went outside!

The next day the new staff member called in sick because I "made her go outside in the heat." She eventually quit due to the "forced" daily outings.

Yes, it is often hot or cold outside, but children need to be outside running and enjoying the weather. We watch the children so that they do not get too hot or too cold. The rule of thumb is to make sure they have water every twenty minutes and to check their faces and hands for redness. We take a thermos of ice water outside and disposable cups. All children are given a cup of water at the same time so we know that each child under our care has had water. We try to keep extra clothing for those who do not have proper clothes for outside. In this state, we may need shorts in the morning but long pants in the afternoon during the winter months.

Some parents also think that we should stay inside during the day during extreme temperatures. Please remember that I am going outside too—not just the children and an assistant. If the temperature is dangerous, I will realize that and take the children inside. As childcare staff, we do not sit in the shade on the playground drinking sodas, eating a snack or chatting with other staff. We move around the playground, interacting with the children and sometimes getting into a game of chase or duck duck goose. Just ten to fifteen minutes twice a day is a lot for the children's growing large motor skills.

## ILLNESSES

During the flu season and with viruses such as H1N1, cleaning is not the only thing that needs to be taken into consideration. We purchased children and adult isolation facemasks for protection against someone who needs to go home but is coughing a lot while waiting to be picked-up. It is easy to place a mask on when we are cleaning up vomit on the floor etc., so the staff members do not breathe the germs. When children are grouped together, they cough and sneeze on each other; therefore daily outside play is very important. Not only is this good for the children to run and play, it is also one of the state guidelines that children go outside daily. We can also open windows to let "germ-bugs" out in the winter while we are outside. Germ-bugs is our way of describing to the young children things we don't see that cause us illness.

Children in a childcare center have lots of illnesses. These include, but are not limited to, conjunctivitis (pink-eye), allergies (food, dust, mold, plants), head lice, ringworm, upper respiratory and ear infections, colds, and runny noses. In our state mandated course, illnesses are discussed quite a lot. Which ones should cause a child to be excluded from the center and which ones can they have but remain in the center? Is a runny nose a reason to send a child home—just a "normal" runny nose or one that is very green (yellow and thick)? The state provides guidelines for this as does each individual center. Remember these are childhood illnesses because by working with young children, you as their teacher, assistant, or caregiver, will probably contact these illnesses too. So, what do you do?

You MUST remember your guidelines and wash your hands frequently. The proper methods of hand washing and diaper changing are other items covered in our state mandated course. In a class I took once, the instructor said that the dirtiest things in a classroom were the children's hands and the second dirtiest were the teacher's. Let's all remember the proper way to wash our hands to prevent contracting more illnesses than we want to. We keep hand sanitizer in our outside "to go" boxes so if we wipe a nose we can sanitize our hands until we go inside to wash them. BUT HAND SANITIZER DOES NOT TAKE THE PLACE OF SOAP AND WATER! As all of us grew up with childhood illnesses and our parents and physicians had different methods for treating them, we have a state-mandated course detailing what can and can't be done to care for a child. For example, I used a vapor rub on my own children's bug bites. For them this took the pain and swelling away rapidly. BUT THIS IS SOMETHING I WOULD NOT DO FOR CHILDREN OTHER THAN MY OWN. Each child's chemistry is different and I could make the child worse by doing this. My state's rules and regulations consist of washing the bite, using an ice pack if needed and calling the parent for any unusual swelling, etc.

A young child could have a fever and the parent/guardian wants us to give them something for this. This may indeed be true but how do we know that the child is not coming down with something else? The medicine that the parent asks us to give the child may not be appropriate for that child's age and by law we as childcare workers may not give any medicine without it being in the original bottle and a doctor's note stating the dosage and times that we are to give this. Some centers in my area do not allow their workers to administer medicine. The child's parent must come to give it or the director/owner gives all medicine.

We must be extremely careful in caring for children in the center. We do not want to add to an illness in anyway. Children bounce back quickly after an illness, but they will get the next thing that is going around. But it appears that children in childcare settings do not get sick as often once they start kindergarten. This may be due to the fact that they have built up their immune system by already having contracted some illnesses.

## COST OF OPERATION

I imagine by now you must think we spend all our money on cleaning supplies. Well, that is just a small amount of the total expense. Expenses in a childcare center are numerous. There are electric, gas, water, and sewer bills to pay. There is the cost of replacement of toys, books, and classroom equipment (chairs, table, easels, etc.). We also need to replace the following at least yearly: crayons, markers, paints, paintbrushes, and a wide assortment of paper for the children to use (construction paper in assorted colors, finger-paint paper, long and short paper). The playground equipment needs replacing or repainting several times—less often when good quality is purchased. The chains on the swings get rusty and new ones are needed, even with tubing over them.

The office supplies are a great expense too. We need paper for the copy machine, ink and also maintenance fees. The adding machine needs tape. A file cabinet with file folders in it to keep children's and staff records is necessary too. We use lots of pencils, pens, highlighters, tape of assorted kinds, staples and staplers, glue, batteries (for radios to take outside) and endless paper clips. These are only a few things that have come to my mind that are constantly used and replaced. There are many others.

All centers furnish some type of food—breakfast, lunch and/or snacks. With this goes the expenses of plates, cups, silverware, napkins, and the cost of the food prepared or purchased for the children. The drink cost is tremendous too. A food bill can run quite high, depending on what is served each month and the number of children in the center. There are food programs available so that a center can get reimbursed for the food that you use if eligible. The necessary forms and the time to fill them out are yet another expense.

Expenses are numerous and many of these continue to increase as the cost of paper products and food rise. A wise kitchen staff/director/owner will shop around for the best buys and use seasonal items in their menus.

## CLEANLINESS

The cleanliness of a childcare center is very important. The children's toys, chairs, tables, etc. MUST BE CLEANED DAILY. Some things may even require cleaning several times a day. If you do not want to clean, then childcare is not for you. The toy and bookshelves, ceiling fans, and light fixtures all must be cleaned. The floors are to be swept and mopped daily and the carpets vacuumed and cleaned. The toilets and sinks must be cleaned many times a day and the diaper pails emptied often. The young boys almost never aim at the toilet accurately, so the back of the toilet, the wall, and the floor must be cleaned frequently. Little girls like to look at themselves in the mirror, so the sink area must be cleaned and dry for them to do this. As the little children that they are, they sure do like to play in the water, so the sink area is always messy, wet, and soapy. The children must wash their hands often, making sure the backs of hands, in between fingers, etc., are washed too and not just quickly slipped under the faucet. We have the children sing their A B C song while washing their hands as this is about the length of time it takes to wash properly. Staff need to wash properly too. We keep a poster in the bathroom by the sink for reminders of "the proper method of hand-washing," another guideline from our state.

The kitchen also needs to be cleaned. Our center furnishes snacks and the staff member who prepares the snack cleans up after all children have eaten and then she takes out the garbage. The children in our center bring their own lunch and we have microwaves available for the staff to warm items up as needed. We clean up after ourselves and a staff member sweeps the floor and takes out the garbage, but we need reminders that the microwave needs to be cleaned out as well as the coffee pot, and all dishes are to be put in the dishwasher and it has to be turned on. This job causes a lot of headache, as no one wants to clean. The kitchen job takes about fifteen to twenty minutes and is something that everyone has had to do. Please remember that daily cleaning is a must for all childcare centers.

The playgrounds also must be cleaned. You will need to check for broken sandbox toys, cars and trucks. These need to be removed and new ones purchased. What about the dirty tissue—where does it go? Is there a garbage can on your playground? Someone needs to empty it too. What about drinks that the staff has had outside (or inside)? These containers need to be kept away during the day—not just left lying around. Who keeps up with the sand on the floor after the children have been outside to play? Who mops up the floor after a toddler has "pottied" on it? Who cleans the carpet when an infant spits up on it? Who cleans the toys after a child has cut their lip on one or when an insect bite has bled when the child scratched it? Some centers are blessed with a cleaning staff that comes in and cleans for them, but many others are not so fortunate. For the safety of the children and the staff, these things cannot be ignored because a staff thinks that it is "not my job." The director needs to ensure that there is a good, regular plan for cleaning at the childcare center.

When new adults walk into our center, they are surprised at how good the center smells. This is only from lots of cleaning all day long. We don't use a lot of sprays and "smell good stuff" due to the rise in children with asthma and allergies. We just use old fashioned cleaning.

As you can sense, the daily operation of a childcare center is expensive. But in order for our children to grow up in a safe and active learning environment, these things are extremely vital. These are things that parents of the children under your care may not notice but if your center is dirty or their children become sick often, this will have parents question what is happening around there.

As a staff member you will want to work in a center that is clean and where you won't be prone to illnesses or to poor work conditions. Please remember that it is everyone's job to keep things clean and safe.

# ᴈ( Chapter 4 )ᴇ
## A Typical Day

This chapter depicts an example of a typical day when I held the job of "Two-year-old Teacher and Assistant Director." The "typical day" was written in the hopes that you will find the rest of the information within this chapter easier to understand. Please do not get discouraged—this was my typical day, not the normal day for a teacher, but it lets you see a bit of what an assistant director's job entails as well. Wearing those dual-hats was a great experience.

I am usually awake at 4:30 a.m., and leave my home at 5:30 a.m. Now, this does not leave any time to clean house or start a load of wash. It means I have time for a couple cups of coffee, a light breakfast, a quick check of my needed lessons and materials for the day and a few minutes to fix my lunch.

Once I arrive at work, a co-worker and I unlock the building, set-up classrooms, change the sign-in sheets for the day, turn on the copy machine, make coffee, fold clothes from last night's wash, and set the air conditioner or heater to the proper setting. We have about twenty minutes to accomplish this. At 6:30 a.m., we unlock the door and the children start arriving. Sometimes they are waiting on the doorstep!

On some days the phone starts ringing as early as 6 a.m. with a staff member who cannot come to work or is running late. Now the fun begins. Who can cover the staff member's classroom? Fortunately, our childcare center believes in a higher child-to-staff ratio than the State requires, which just means when someone calls in sick it might be that a teacher does not have her assistant that day. Occasionally, we have someone already out on vacation, or convalescent leave due to surgery, or a family member who is sick. This means a little creativity is needed to keep all rooms covered. This is a challenge that I go through many times a month, sometimes weekly. It is one part of my job that I really enjoy doing—you can't plan ahead for this (unless your center has several substitutes on hand—which few do). The adjustments must be done on the spot to make sure that you can legally keep your doors open.

The changes about who will be in which room sometimes place other staff in bad humor. Some staff might be upset because they don't have their class assistant today and others might be upset that someone is out again.

HERE IS WHAT HAPPENED ON<br>MONDAY, MAY 20<sup>th</sup>

Our director is out for the next two days, Monday and Tuesday, but will return on Wednesday. She has sent all the staff a note about being away, asking everyone to help each other as needed, and to remember that I am the Assistant Director.

I had a nice, relaxed weekend and was looking forward to a great start to this new week. We had a new staff member with four years of toddler experience starting, and an interview scheduled for Thursday with another potential staff member. Things were finally looking up for the toddler class. I had planned on finishing the painting of the classroom and organizing the necessary paperwork on Saturday, so the classroom would be ready for the new staff.

Our subs for the infant room were due in at 8 a.m. and had not arrived by 8:45 a.m. I went to the phone to call them (maybe they forgot what time they were due) and there was no dial tone. Fortunately, I had my fully charged cell phone. When I called the phone company, I was put on hold for twenty minutes. They assured me that our phone would be fixed by closing. I said, "Please, as soon as possible, we are a childcare center and MUST have phone service."

Two other employees who were to work a split shift were not here either. I called and left messages for them. So now it was time to re-adjust the staff, so that we were once again back in ratio. This done, I spoke with each staff member about changes. Then one staff member told me she was turning in her resignation. I asked her why. She had personal issues but thought with the summer off (she requested this earlier last week), that maybe she would return in the fall, but now she wasn't sure. I asked her to wait until our director returned on Wednesday, since the summer off might be a possibility. She agreed. Now off to my classroom—needless to say, some of my lessons for the day were not done.

The rest of the morning went smoothly—only a little unsettling for me, as the phone still was not operating. The director and her parents stopped by the center on their way to Atlanta around noon with the checkbook and last minute advice.

The afternoon was fairly quiet—but still no phone. One child had diarrhea during naptime, so I called the parent. Then, I made the copies of the latest shigellosis bacteria news from the Health Department to send home with all children and one for each staff member. An outbreak in our county prompted all parents to be notified of the information. This information is important to parents to know what the policy is for sending children home, should it be necessary, how to have them tested and when they can return to school.

I started the notices for immunization and physicals that were due, when the infant room had a child vomit. The phone was still out, so again I used my cell phone to contact the parent. Well, back to the notices. Ooops, at 4 p.m., the 3 p.m. staff member had not arrived. Time to re-adjust the staff again.

Once all my paperwork was completed and delivered to the classrooms, I talked to our new toddler employee about the paperwork she needed to finish, and about her shoes. Our center had a dress code that shoes must be closed-toed, with a strap across the back. (See section on Dress Code.)

Then, a parent came in and wanted to talk with me. She and her husband are splitting up and he took the kids.... This ended up with the office doors closed and her crying hysterically. Listening to parents takes priority sometimes, no matter what is going on elsewhere.

The phone still is not working at 5:30 p.m. I called the phone company again—they could not find a work order—just great!! The woman places us on a priority for the next day. I made sure to remind myself to recharge my cell phone that night.

I arrived home at 6:30 p.m. First, I called the infant staff member, who could not work that day due to her car not starting, to see if she was planning on working the next day. She said the car still wasn't running but she was going to borrow a friend's car and assured me she would return to work.

I began to relax, thinking that my Tuesday was set. HA! HA! HA! A phone call from the infant teacher, told me something different. She had a family emergency but would work until paychecks arrived around noon. That was good for me—she works until 2:15 normally, so this coverage will be easy. The assistant to the two-year-old class could cover during naptime when I was there.

I decided to check on my cell phone, as I had limited daytime minutes. I needed to find out how much extra this was costing me. The woman assured me that if I went over my allowed minutes, it was ONLY $.40 a minute. However, she was glad I called, as a new plan started that month (really!) and I could get extra daytime minutes for only $4.00 extra per month. As an assistant to the director, I know a little math. I quickly told her to sign me up! I didn't know if the phone would be fixed at work the following day or not.

My supper that night was easy to prepare, just tuna sandwiches with boiled eggs. What a great husband I have to enjoy a simple meal! I ironed us both something to wear the next day and finished watching "A Flight from Phoenix" and then off to bed. I knew tomorrow was payday and fog was expected. This meant the checks might arrive late as we use a company in Atlanta and our checks are flown to Mobile—weather permitting they might arrive on time. If not, a few staff might get jittery about whether they were going to get their check before leaving for the day.

This is just one of many "typical" days for me. Do you see the problems that directors have to be able to handle? A daily dose of patience, prayer, and guidance is required.

## WORK ATTIRE

The work attire for a childcare center is loose, comfortable, but professional. Wow! How do you accomplish this?

In order to get down to a child's level, you must have on clothing that moves with you. If it is too tight, you just can't get down to the level of a two-year-old or crawl on the floor with a one-year-old. For this, nice slacks are more comfortable than leggings and more professional than jeans. Young children require a lot of running after, and you find yourself standing on your feet a lot, so comfortable shoes like sneakers are great to wear. Low, flat-heeled shoes look good with a skirt or dress. When you run across the playground after a child who has fallen or needs your help, shoes that do not have backs on them sometimes fall off your feet, either hindering your quickness to help a child or causing injury to yourself. This becomes an insurance issue if a staff is injured due to not wearing proper shoes.

Some centers have uniforms for staff to wear. This makes it easy for a parent or a new child to recognize that you belong and are someone to go to for help. Your work attire does not need to be name brand and cost big bucks. We do a lot of painting and numerous times the paint goes through our clothes, even with an apron on. Sometimes the "washable" paint does not wash out. We use a bleach solution for cleaning that sometimes gets on our clothes, discoloring them. Many discount clothing stores are available for you to purchase good clothing at lower prices. Before purchasing new clothes, please check to see if the childcare center that you are employed at has a dress code.

Some staff members prefer to wear smocks in their classrooms, removing it before going home. This way their clothes remain clean. When you are holding little ones during the day, perhaps someone crying, changing a diaper, or assisting someone in their cutting skills, you will brush up against them or the food they are eating. I personally do not like wearing a smock. I feel that if I do, that I project an image that I don't want anyone to touch me, that I am too good to get dirty. So I just bring a change of clothes to keep in my car.

In this section, I would like to remind both men and women to limit the cologne or perfume that they wear. Remember that little ones may have asthma and respiratory infections, and the wearing of strong perfume or cologne makes it even harder for them to breathe.

## PAPERWORK

Where do I begin on this subject? Paperwork—what is paperwork in a childcare setting? To start with, each child needs a registration form with his or her parent's/guardian's information on it in case we need to call. The children must have an immunization record and a physical form—their physician or the health department provides these to the parent. These forms must be kept up-to-date and it is our job to keep track of this. In the classroom, a teacher needs a file on each child. Included in the file should be date of enrollment, medical history, authorization of who can pick-up the child, and the child's date of birth. If you are keeping track of height and weight, then another form is kept on this.

What about the diaper changes, bowel movements and the child's eating habits? Yes, you guessed it—more paperwork!

A letter should go home monthly to the parents, explaining what their child will be doing during the upcoming month and any special events that will be happening. Along with this letter, we include a calendar that can be placed on the refrigerator to keep track of these events. Please keep in mind when furnishing this information to the parents, that there may be children who live with mom this week and dad next week. We need to make two sets of this information for those cases, so that both parents have the same information. Remember, we are not to judge, and by giving one set only, we are judging who we think is the better or more responsible parent.

The lesson plans need to be written to show that we do indeed have a plan for what we are doing. Our lessons plans should not only cover the fun things that we are doing but why we are doing them. What is our purpose for introducing a new finger play, for example? Is it to show that we know lots of finger plays or that the children will develop more small motor skills and improve language development?

We need reasons for the things that we do in our classrooms. So the most likely place to start is with evaluations of each child in our care. What can the children already do, what stage are they in, do they have any language skills, and can they get from here to there? These are just a few of the questions that you need to answer when evaluating the children's skills. The evaluations are done twice a year in most centers. I like to do mine the first three weeks of school, make my lesson plans according to the needs of each child, and do another evaluation in two months. This keeps me aware of any potential problems that each child may be having and to see if my lessons are providing what each child needs. I send home evaluations twice a year, unless more are needed. When a parent conference is needed, I have all my evaluations to fall back on. Evaluations and other documentation that have been written over a period of time carry more weight than something off the top of your head. Remember that it is the process, not the product, that is the learning tool.

We have paperwork to do regarding our assistants, caregivers, teachers and directors. We do fingerprint background checks, past employment checks, fill-out tax forms on all employees and document any benefits or raises that are due to them. We have paperwork on fire drills, including when we have them, the time of day, the staff-to-child ratio for that day, and how long it took to clear the building. There is even paperwork on all visits by Licensing or the Department of Health, and on any maintenance that needs to be done. We do have a lot of paperwork.

## DAILY ROUTINE

Many people ask me, "What do you do with 16 children who are two years old from 6:30 a.m. to 6:00 p.m.!?" A routine is usually set (not in stone) by the lead teacher of the room or by the director/owner. This requires that each staff in a childcare center participate. Now it is up to all staff in that classroom to help keep to the routine as best as possible.

I remember one day when I worked at the church-based childcare center when I was late for chapel with the Pastor. I had started the morning out with no problem. Then just as we were going out the door, a young two-year-old who was in potty training, decided he needed to go NOW and another had a bowel movement in her pants. We waited for one to get changed and then I proceeded to take the others to chapel. We try to keep to our routine, but at times we must be flexible.

Children expect and need a routine. But when the sun is shining and there are lots of roly poly bugs in the weeds, the children just want to watch them in lieu of the great lesson that you worked on all weekend. What do you do? It is time for that lesson of the day, but the children will get more out of the bugs in the weeds than any lesson. The hands-on learning is great and your lesson can wait for a day when you need a fill-in.

Children need to know when it is mealtime, naptime, outdoor playtime, and bathroom time. They like predictability and normally we, the staff, do too. Some children will get very cranky when their routine changes. Routines sometimes need to be changed for the safety of all children. During these times, we must prepare the children under our care for any changes.

An example of this is when a child under my care came to school one morning later than usual. When we finished eating our breakfast, we would go to our room for circle time and lessons. This was when the child arrived. He kept telling me, "No" that he did not want to participate in circle. He usually enjoyed this time, so I asked, "Why not?" The child replied, "Cause we have to go to breakfast first."

Well, in his eyes he was right, but the other children had already been there and now it was time for our circle. What does one do? I knew a temper tantrum was on it way, so I took the clock down that we used for Hickory Dickory Dock and showed him on the "Daily Routine" paper, that breakfast was at 8 a.m. and now it was 8:45 a.m. I explained that his daddy had gotten up late and he had arrived at school later than usual. I asked him if he ate with daddy and when he replied, "Yes" I reminded him that he had breakfast with daddy today, and not with his friends at school. He said, "Oh, okay!" Boy, was I glad that we were all okay—no tempers and he remembered that he did have breakfast sometimes at home, like cartoon day and church day. Routines keep the peace sometimes too.

In conclusion, you see that a typical day is far from that. Each day is different and full of challenges. We are on our feet most of the day, supervising young children and providing a safe learning atmosphere for them. We have little to no time to chitchat with fellow employees, except on our breaks. Our job is unlike any other—the children must come first.

We must remember this during the day, parents will bring their child to school late or forget a needed item, but it is not our place to judge them. We must try to put ourselves in their shoes. Your "typical day" will reward you with more patience, understanding of others, flexibility, and nurturing than you ever thought possible. Think and act in a positive manner and you will reap instant rewards!

# ﹎ Chapter 5 ﹎
## Teacher's Collections

A teacher's collection contains the items that she or he needs to survive daily. The collections vary according to age groups of children and teacher's preferences.

I have been in the childcare profession for over two decades, and I have numerous collections. Other teachers may have less than I do or more. I would like to share my collections with you. It will make you more aware of how different collections add to the daily curriculum.

I am a hands-on teacher and feel a need for all my collections. You may be asking, "Why is a teacher's collection in a book about childcare?" Teachers' collections are essential to daily survival in the classroom. These are the tools that she or he guides the children with, the things they pull out on a rainy day and the items that are used to enhance the lessons.

At the beginning of each year, I have planned what themes, colors, shapes, etc., that I will be using for the entire school year. Sometimes it is similar to what I have previously used and sometimes I have added new ones or current ones that the new children under my care are interested in. As teachers have a limited budget (remember those low wages), we go to numerous garage sales and join book clubs to get teaching books, reading books and other materials at discount prices. We also look for various items around the house that we can use in the classroom setting.

## BOOKS

When I first started my teaching job, I found that the young children under my care were like little sponges. They just absorb anything and everything! They love to hear new and old stories. How many times have I read and used the flannel board for "Brown Bear, Brown Bear"! This is a great book for color recognition and sequencing.

Of course, my book collection needed to grow. So, I joined several book clubs and started receiving books monthly. I purchased books to be used in my theme units, focusing on books to help with colors, shapes, numbers, and the alphabet. My book selection also needed books on holidays, and a variety of other topics.

I found out that I needed books to help children adjust to their first day of school, to help with a new baby arriving at their home, and to help with fears. The books from my book clubs provided a lot of this information for me, however, now I needed books for the multi-cultural lessons too. I found a trip to the local children's bookstore gave me more than I could ever need. What a find! This store has been in my hometown for many years and only through a workshop did I find out about it (another value of the workshops available to childcare workers).

Along with books to read to the children to enhance my monthly themes, I felt I needed books to help me teach. Some of these I was able to purchase through the book clubs. I also used catalogs and stores for teachers in my town. A few of my favorites are listed in the back of this book. In order to use themes to the best of my ability, I ordered lots of teaching books with ideas and projects and the reasons for using them.

As I attend each workshop that is available for the age of children that I work with, I have purchased numerous books and materials on various subjects. A few of these subjects include block play, misbehavior, autism, ADD, ADHD, speech and hearing problems, ways to arrange a classroom, developmental stages, and effective communication between teacher and parent. I use all of these books in my daily work with young children. The books help me to plan my lessons, as the topics become things that I have at my fingertips. I also can usually find something in my books to help me assist a parent, child or another staff member with a problem or a new idea.

Books provide a lot of learning experience and language development. This is why I make the Scholastic book club available for parents to choose books for their child to read at home. I have listed the address in the Index. A monthly selection is available for parents to purchase and the teacher of the child's class receives bonus points to order books free for her/his class. What a worthwhile project!

Now, where to store all of these books? A natural choice is at school, where the books are handy should I come across a problem. But I soon realized that I was taking books home with me to re-read, so now some are at work, some are at home, and a lot are in my car (in case I need them at both home and school).

To organize my collections, I place themes together by the month that I will use each. I use a plastic tub to store items in—one tub for every two months. Where do I store all of these plastic tubs? In my garage at home, of course! Now my tubs have grown, and I have twelve plastic tubs for monthly themes and a few for craft items (assorted colors of yarn, ribbons, laces, fabrics, buttons, etc.). Some of my books are in these for monthly themes and others are marked for teacher/parent use. There are not enough bookshelves to handle all of my books.

## MUSIC

A collection of music is a <u>must</u>. The learning that takes place through music with the children's social skills, motor skills, language skills, and cognitive skills cannot be compared to other areas of my collections.

We need a lot of shakers to accompany our music—homemade ones are great! We use empty small soda bottles and assorted small items to fill them with. The bottles need to be clean and dry, both inside and out. The children are given a variety of objects to place inside their bottles (great for hand-eye coordination and small muscle control). These items could be pinto beans, navy beans, butterbeans, colored popcorn, or feathers. When the child fills the container about half-full, then it is time for the teacher to hot-glue the tops on so the tops cannot be removed. The children then can decorate the outside of their bottle. When all are ready, we put on assorted music—fast, slow, marching, or tiptoeing. What fun we have in our band! These shakers can also be made with paper plates or cups.

The use of colored scarves is the ultimate fun! These are hard to find, but can be made using very lightweight fabric. We can throw them in the air and watch them fall to slow music or toss them to fast music trying to keep them in the air. The concept of fast/slow along with the sound is a great learning experience.

In addition to CDs and cassette tapes, you must have a few records. Do you know that some children have never seen a record? When a group of my two-year-olds were watching the record go around and around, one of them put his little hand on it to stop the record and then lifted his hand to let it play again. What an experience they had!

Many children's books come with CDs or cassette tapes so that the children can listen to the book, if someone is not available to read to them. This is great for the children to practice listening, especially if you quiz them about what they heard afterwards. But just listening to music isn't enough. The children should be encouraged to be interactive whenever possible. We use as many musical instruments as our budget allows. The playing of drums, bongos, sticks, triangles, and maracas are so enjoyable that the children want to play with them daily, so we incorporate them into their own area in the center for use. Most of these instruments can be made. Some of the books in the Index have directions for making an assortment of musical instruments out of stuff around the house.

Please include daily music time with young children. Add to your collection often, by bringing a variety of music into your classroom. It will be rewarding to the children, aiding in both artistic and motor development and into increasing their language skills. Singing songs is just as important to children as hearing music, playing musical instruments, and dancing to music. We sing our ABCs, nursery rhyme songs, silly songs, ones with motions and even a few made-up songs. Sometimes when the children are outside on the swings they are singing songs. I overheard one small child singing on a swing who made up her own song based on some of the words we had used in class before. She was singing, "Where is Miss Peggy, where is Miss Peggy, I don't know, I don't know." She kept singing this most of the play period, even when she saw me walk by multiple times. She was being creative and joyful.

## PUPPETS

What child does not enjoy puppets? They all love to use finger puppets and hand puppets of all shapes and sizes. Puppets can be a part of a lot of learning activities, such as showing how one eats and how we feel and how to touch our friends. Sometimes children cannot express their problems to others but with a puppet they feel more comfortable and less threatened.

Puppets can help teach children their shapes and colors. These can be made with felt for finger puppets and used daily. What fun can be had naming our puppets! Mr. Orange suddenly appears, and we look around the room for something the same color as he is. How much fun we have trying to find lots of orange things for him to play with! Sometimes Ms. Blue is sad and only wants to be left alone, but we can usually perk her up with a blue blanket and when we find blue bunny hiding under a blanket, she usually starts to feel better. Mr. Red loves to play with the shape of a stop sign and to ride on a red fire truck. Our shape and color puppets have lots of fun together as our shapes are finger puppets and our colors are puppets on a tongue depressors. They like to stay busy hopping here and there.

As puppets come in assorted sizes, we must have all types in our classroom. I started off with basic puppets of animals. All children enjoy cats, dogs, cows, pigs, and then I added new ones monthly. We now have all farm animals, most zoo animals, all pets and some insects. What fun it is to use the caterpillar puppet, watching it cocoon (turned inside-out) and then emerge into a butterfly (open outside). We watch our multi-colored bird that has a hidden chirper inside suddenly "talk."

Not all puppets need to be made commercially. Children love to make puppets. We make at least one puppet a month. For our farm unit, we might make a pig. We used a paper pattern of a pig and glued it to an empty spool of thread. For a unit on Fall/Halloween, we made pumpkins on toilet paper tubes and sang the song "Five Little Pumpkins." The month of November brought out Pilgrims and Indians made of felt. The list goes on and on with making puppets.

Many books are available for making and using puppets. You may check in your local library, stores in your town, and some catalog companies (in the Index) also provide sources for puppet making. We have books on how to make finger puppets, how to make stand-alone puppets, string puppets, and just-for-fun puppets. I would recommend that unless you are very talented and have lots of free time, that you purchase books or find online resources on making simple puppets. Some are very beautiful but require lots of time to make. The children need simple ones to make. For instance, cut two pieces of felt into whatever shape you wish (cookie cutters are great to use as patterns); younger children can put glue around the edges while older children can stitch the edges together with yarn. Then they can decorate with bits of lace, buttons, and other age-appropriate materials.

To go with our "Hungry Caterpillar" book, I used a big sock with a face drawn on and made picture cutouts with the hole in the center for my sock-caterpillar to eat his way through. What fun this is as I read the story and each child can feed the caterpillar.

We made a set of puppets for "Goldilocks and the Three Bears." We used yellow doll hair for Goldilocks and assorted colored felt for her body. The face features could be made with markers, buttons, or additional felt. (Check your other collections of "stuff".) I used a glue gun for mine but the children use regular white glue. Another puppet set that is used often is "The Three Pigs." This set provides lots of learning on sizes and sequencing. We have taken felt board patterns and made stick puppets with tongue depressors for the story of "Brown Bear, Brown Bear." Sometimes we even use paper plates for a moveable mouth or make a puppet with assorted sizes of plates and cups.

Besides stick puppets and finger puppets, another fun puppet is the mitt (glove) puppet. These are available in stores and catalogs to purchase, however, they are simple to make. All that is needed for one is a garden glove, and since gloves come in pairs, you will be able to make two puppets. You will need felt and assorted color and sizes of pom-poms. (Look in your craft collection.) The one I use the most is "Old MacDonald." I glued a felt barn on to the palm of the glove and my assorted pom-poms and felt animals were glued to the fingertips. These make wonderful gifts for children, too!

A stage is helpful but not necessary. A cardboard box with a sheet over it, a shelf unit, a doorway or even a few chairs grouped together make scenery easy to set-up. If it takes too much time to get ready, the children will lose interest and move on to something else. Many commercial stages are available for doorways and tabletops as well as full-size stages. Some of these are available through the catalog companies listed in the Index.

Many parents over the years have given me puppets for gifts. My treasured ones are the set of five (owl, elephant, bird, mouse and ferret) from Sarah and her mom. Sarah was in my class for three years. She arrived as a ten-month-old in my toddler class and then in my two-year-old class for the next two years, due to her birthday. Sarah's mother knew of my love of puppets and wanted me to have these treasures that she had found. They are still treasured by me many years later.

Now that all these puppets have been collected—where do you store them? As I feel children need puppets available daily, we have a plastic dishpan filled with at least one puppet for every child and teacher in the classroom to use. Some that are used only for lessons are on a peg-shelf that a friend made for me. Others are scattered around the room. For example, the block center has community helper puppets and in the library center we have the Three Pigs, the farm glove and assorted ones to just hold while we read. I still have some in my garage and one or two in the car. I never want to be without a puppet around me.

Once you start using puppets to help children gain the following skills, I feel that you will never be without a puppet close by again, just like me.

Puppets can help children:

1. Explore with shapes and sizes in science activities.
2. Increase communication and listening to others to gain language skills.
3. Encourage use of sensory skills.
4. Develop small and large muscle skills.
5. Increase use of hand-eye coordination.
6. Be creative with music movement.
7. Gain confidence in talking with others in play-acting to improve social skills.

I have given you just a few examples of puppets and the learning that can come out of them. Just be yourself and enjoy every teachable moment with your children. Please add to your puppet collection for the enjoyment of all!

## HOUSEHOLD STUFF

A new book arrived from a book club I joined and guess what—it is filled with things to do with "junk" from around the house. So, now all of my family and friends save empty spools of thread, toilet paper tubes, oatmeal containers, coffee cans, yogurt containers, buttons, and plastic containers from margarine, cream cheese, peanut butter, etc. Now, where do I put all of this? Again, some is at school, but most is at home and let's not forget the car in case time allows for something else to do.

Some of the ideas for these recycled items are:

1. Empty spools of thread make great holders for sponge painting. Take the spool, cut a square of cardboard two inches larger than the sponge shape, and glue onto the spool, then glue on the sponge. Now the child has something to hold onto in order to stamp paint, and it won't drip when turned upside down.

2. Paper tubes are good for puppet making, and good for making binoculars as well. Take two tubes and tape them together, and attach yarn for a holder.

3. Oatmeal, coffee and salt containers make great drums and miniature baskets for Easter.

4. Yogurt containers can be used for paint buckets.

5. Greeting cards can be made into baskets by lacing them together with yarn or ribbon. You can make picture books by lacing them together, or just cut out the pictures to glue.

6. Lids to plastic containers can be made into tree decorations with old Christmas cards (yes I collect those too). Cut out the card to the lid size, glue to the lid and decorate. Use ribbon or yarn for hanging.

7. Tuna and pet food cans can be used for a vase for flowers for a table decoration.

8. Shoe boxes can be made into cars, buses, animal cages, pull toys, shadow boxes, and doll or puppet beds.

9. Phone books covered with contact paper are great to make an obstacle course. You may use them in a single line for a walking path. These are great to strengthen arms when stacking. The little children love to pick them up and move them from one place to another. These make a great rainy day activity and can be used in the block center for making buildings.

These ideas are ones collected over the years of teaching, through workshops, from my peers, or from ideas in books I have purchased. I have listed some of the books in the Index.

Collections of "stuff" are very important tools for teachers. We can find a use for almost anything. Our only problem is storage. Please don't think of us as slobs when you see our cars with a plastic container of items—we just need all that stuff!

## YARD SALES

I have always enjoyed going to yard sales to find the perfect something that I didn't have. The variety of things available for reasonable prices is limitless. So, when I first started teaching, I knew that I needed to go to more yard sales to find things for classroom use.

As you remember, I have already decided the theme units that I will be using all year. So, when I run across something that I could use in a few months, I of course purchase it for that unit. I enjoy using the real object versus a toy one. I feel the children under my care learn to value this object as they usually have one at home. We use it in the proper manner and then they will respect the object at home, too.

Sometimes I go to yard sales to find one certain thing. One year I was in search of a scale, either one for the bathroom, one to check postage, or a scale used in the kitchen. I wanted it for our Pre-K teacher, who started off a new school year by checking the height and weight of each child. What a math lesson they can have by finding something else in the classroom that weighs as much as they do—or to find out how much something weighs versus something else. So, a few old scales were needed from a yard sale adventure.

When I go to yard sales and find interesting things for themes, of course I buy them. Who could resist old flannel shirts, jeans and hats to wash and put away for a scarecrow for our garden when we do a farm unit? Cow slippers or adult high heels are perfect for the dress up corner and small suitcases and backpacks can be used on "airplane" trips. What a find, when I came across empty berry baskets. My children love to weave ribbon into them or fill them with Easter grass and make a bird's nest. Just dipping them into paint to use for assorted painting techniques is another option. The endless array of plastic flowers I find allows us to have an instant flowerbed or makes wonderful table decorations for our tea parties.

When spring/summer approaches and we are outside more, the children love to play in the sandbox. I think Florida children have outgrown a sand bucket and shovel. Our children seem to like assorted things like muffin pans, big spoons, plastic molds, assorted plastic drinking cups, empty plastic saltshakers, etc. I even need old plastic place mats, as they like "cooking" and "serving" their special imaginary dish of the day in the sandbox. I have found that metal spoons, pots, and pans make lots of noise and are the ones wanted most, but in Florida we must remember that on summer days these get hot in the sun and could burn little hands.

After Halloween, I always go to several yard sales to look for old costumes and apparel. These make great inexpensive items for our dress-up corner. Sometimes, I even find an ugly mask to show the children that it is fake, and not something to be afraid of next year. I can find capes and angel wings for our Christmas program and bats and spiders for our insect unit.

Throughout the year, I am able to find lots of fast food restaurant toys. These small toys are in much demand with the children. Every child must have a closet full, even when their parents get rid of some. I use the toys for outside table play, for inside rice/sand table play or for just holding onto. Sometimes these toys are $0.25 each, but usually I can get a bag full for $0.10 each. I can put these toys in an empty ice cream bucket and the children will play for hours. These make a great rainy day activity so I keep some hidden away for just that.

Please remember that in searching at yard sales for "stuff" for your classroom, be sure to look at the edges of items, making sure they are not cracked or chipped. The items need to be washed and re-washed for usage in the classroom. We need to be very careful with pre-owned items that we bring into a classroom setting. We should also check the list for any recalled toys.

## INSECTS

What are insects doing in a collection chapter and why would you want insects in a classroom setting? Don't we have enough to do without "bugs" too? These are questions that I am sure you must be asking about now. I hope to show you the importance of these creatures.

There has not been a day that has gone by in my years of teaching that we have not stopped to look at or try to catch a bug. On the way to breakfast at the childcare center where I worked for years, we went from one building to another using a short sidewalk outside. Sometimes we would see a spider that has just spun a beautiful web. The class would stop to look. In the lunchroom, a fly might disturb us, or when on the playground we might find a roly poly. The children have a great interest in bugs, and ask, "What do they do?" and "Where do they go?" For this reason alone, we should discuss insects.

My spring/summer theme is the birth of life, with insects and frogs. What are a few things needed for this? We must watch caterpillars emerge as butterflies; we must have an incubator to see a baby chick hatch from an egg; and of course we must watch lizards, frogs, and turtles move around.

What does this mean for me? Many assorted sizes of aquariums, an incubator and several large, empty pickle jars for earthworms, crickets, etc. Also needed is some type of lamp (clip-on preferred) to keep the baby chicks warm after hatching and small containers for food and water (butter or yogurt containers work best) for the "critters" to eat and drink from.

Let's not forget our sand, sun, and sea unit. We need plastic insects, starfish, assorted sizes of seashells, seaweed and driftwood. It sounds like a trip to the beach is needed! And off to another yard sale in October for old swimming pools to make a beach, to hold the plastic fish, whales and sharks, with toilet paper tubes for palm trees.

By searching for stories and objects to teach the children, my insect collection has grown. Our classroom now has assorted bugs for our flannel board, bug puppets, bug books, and crawling bugs in assorted cages.

We not only have hands-on science lessons but are given time to watch what happens when a pickle jar of dirt and earthworms becomes a winding road. These experiments lead children to respect things in our world, as well as understand more about safety. As we learn more about insects, we learn not to touch them, as some like to bite us (like ants and snakes, even thought they are very colorful).   Some of our children could sit and watch bugs all day!

One day I had to put our aquarium that held "baby" frogs, "mama" frogs, "daddy" frogs, and lizards outside. We had just finished giving the frogs some live crickets to eat when it was outside playtime. Bad idea on my part. No one wanted to go outside, because they wanted to watch the frogs and lizards <u>eat</u> the crickets. So out went the aquarium to the playground, so we could see who ate most, the big frog or the funny-looking lizard.

We must make time to discuss insects as they are part of our lives each and every day. The learning that takes place is so important, not only the name and habitat of each insect, but also the knowledge of taking care of one of nature's little creatures. The responsibility of caring for one will help with a family pet later.

# ঙ( Chapter 6 )ঙ
## Interaction

Interaction with children seems to enhance my life. While there are many families without young children, I cannot imagine what my life would be without any. As my daughter and son are grown, the time I spend each day with the young children under my care and my own young grandson is very important and rewarding to me.

I remember a few years ago when I was working a split shift, I arrived at school before the children, and took a break while they had a nap. Then I returned and worked until the last child left for the day.

When I went to a straight shift, the children could not understand why or where I was going. One child said, as I was getting my bag and purse, "Where are you going, Ms. Peggy?" I replied, "I am going home." The child said, "No, this is your home." To them it was my home and sometimes I think I am at work more than at home too. But I can't help but think what a wonderful place it is to be!

This chapter explains how my job does not leave enough energy to socialize with others and how others, not in this field, question what I do and why I stay in this field.

## TIME FRAME

As we have seen in Chapter 2, the responsibility of a teacher in a childcare center is tremendous. We wake up early to start our household chores, get our family members off to their jobs or school, and check to make sure we have all our lesson materials for the day. This in itself leaves us wanting a caffeine break as soon as we arrive at work.

Instead, we sweetly greet our parents and children—trying to remember the details that the parents share with us about each child, like who will be getting picked up early or late, etc. All of this is done while settling a wrestling match between two children who want to be the line leader.

The day moves uphill or downhill with small plateaus in between. At lunchtime you notice someone forgot their lunch, another fell asleep at the table without eating, and your assistant decides she needs to go home as her sinuses are bothering her.

When we finally leave for the day, we have our own groceries to buy, bills to prepare to mail, and supper to cook. Now, our dishes are done, wash from this morning is placed in the dryer, children and/or husband are settled and it is 9:00 p.m. Tomorrow is another day and we will try to accomplish things that have not been done today.

## UNDERSTANDING THE FIELD

Many friends I have do not understand what I do and most do not understand WHY I DO IT!

Besides a strong caring interest that I have in children, I have a strong passion for sewing and quilting. I have a sewing group of friends (Joyce, Rose and Margaret) who come every Saturday to my home to sew. Occasionally we work on our sewing but mostly we work on catching up with each other's week. When it is my "turn" they look at me strangely—but less then they used to, because after over twenty years they think they have heard everything. Of course, as a professional, NO NAMES of staff, children or parents ARE EVER mentioned in our conversations.

It is amazing to them the things that occur during the day or week. It's almost like a soap opera—they can't wait until the next sewing group to see what has happened. But friends who work in this field understand, sympathize, and usually can top any story you can tell.

I look upon us in the profession as a "dying breed." Many of today's young people do not have the same desire to join us. I believe the low wages and the amount of work involved keep many away. Each article I read on the importance of "birth through three years old" makes me feel that I am indeed an important part of today's society. I may not be wealthy in money or have friends who understand what I do, but I am wealthy in hugs, kisses and gratitude from parents and my friends who support me in my daily adventures of life as a preschool teacher. What more could a person hope for?

## QUESTIONS MOST FREQUENTLY ASKED

Some of the questions that I have been asked over the past twenty years include:

1. *Why did you want to become a teacher?*

First, when I started the only thing that I knew were children. Second, I love the expressions children make, their love for life and abundance of energy. Being around them seems to keep me young. The saying, "if it ain't broke, don't fix it" applies to me. I have been in this profession so long now that it has become second nature.

2. *Why have you stayed in the profession so long?*

I don't know. I have tried numerous times to leave but my heart keeps me here. God has a plan for us all—mine must be to remain in my profession.

3. *Aren't you burned out yet?*

What is burned out? The times I feel that I do not understand a child or parent, or have the patience to handle the situation then I hope God will give me his guidance to follow. I try to enjoy my weekends and holidays to the fullest—to realize there is a life besides my "job" and to discuss my problems with my peers. In this way, for me there is no burn out. With lots of prayer that I can do all I can to help today's parents cope with their problems, I hope to continue in my field for many more years.

4. *Don't you ever want to make more money?*

It might be nice to have lots of money—to be able to buy what you want when you want it. But when the money runs out and the stuff you bought wears out, what do you have left? I have a little money and years of wonderful memories of the young children and their parents who I have met.

5. *Don't you get tired of kids hanging on you all day?*

Yes, there are times I want to be left alone but <u>never</u> do I feel this in the presence of a child. The warmth from that last hug of the day remains with me until the next child comes "hanging on."

6. *Aren't you afraid of catching something?*

Over the years, I have "caught" a few things. Most colds, sinus infections, bronchitis, etc., I would have "caught" anyway if I ever left my house. However, I have "caught" many smiles over the years that I would have missed had I not became a teacher.

7. *Why do you put up with being hit and bit?*

I don't "put up" with being hit or bit. My choice of becoming a teacher of preschool children is my own to deal with. Children of this age do not intend to harm or hurt others. It is age-appropriate for them to bite or hit from time to time. My job is to successfully help them develop language skills to express their wants and to allow them to "bite" pretzels, crackers, and chewable toys or to "hit" with the hammers on the pounding benches or the keys of the musical toys in appropriate ways.

8. *Don't you want to clobber parents sometimes when they are not caring enough for their kids?*

There are times that I get frustrated with parents, yes. But I not only help the child but also the parent and/or family unit to see an easier way to deal with their emotions and frustrations of the day. If I cannot help them, I will find books, articles, or another professional to answer their problems. We must remember that parents are human too!

9. *How can you stand the noise?*

What is noise—a loud airplane in the sky, a motorcycle revved up, radio station static, the sound of a lawn mower, someone crunching ice? A child is joyful music to my ears and a classroom of two-year-olds is the symphony playing.

10. *Are you insane?*

I guess I am! I enjoy going to work each day. One reason is that there are no two days alike; therefore, it is not boring. I always look forward to whatever problems the day will bring for me to solve!

I could never sit all day behind a desk or in front of a computer. I don't have the strength to drive a truck or to be a construction worker. I would feel bored by working a cash register. But, I can sit all day cuddling a child and I do have the strength to push a child on the swing during the play period and the strength of patience.

I do not mind the endless reading of the same book over and over—it is never boring. My "insanity" unfortunately is not contagious as there are too few of us in this most rewarding profession.

The interaction with children should be a cautious, positive one. We must remember that children are fragile little creatures. As adults, our daily life has many stressful situations and our reactions, sometimes are not what they should be. Positive guidance goes a long way.

SPEAK TO OTHERS (children included) AS YOU WANT TO BE SPOKEN TO.

# Chapter 7
## Memories

All of the memories included in this chapter are real ones. Each one has taught me things about myself as a teacher and as a person. Some have surprised me with the things that children say, while others remind me of the importance of my profession.

Each child is unique and comes from a different background—some have two parents, some are from single parent homes, others are raised by their grandparents. It does not matter who the primary caregiver is to the child. As long as there is an abundance of love and guidance, children will become unique, productive adults with lots of experience along the way to share with their family.

I will try to describe the settings for each memory so you can visualize as you read. Some people say, "You must be there to appreciate this." I hope to provide you with enough information that you will feel that you were there or maybe you have been there already.

I have had so many memories over the past twenty years, but some easily became my favorites. In addition to several stories, I have included some "famous" quotes. I am sure if you work around children long enough you will experience some of the same. Some will make you laugh and others might make you cry. Please enjoy!

My children were raised in the early 1970s. I feel very fortunate that I had the pleasure to get up early with my husband, Joe, see him off to work and then go about my daily housework. When my children decided to get up (usually around 8 a.m.), then my day really began! What fun to see the sleepy-headed children yawn and stretch, waking up to a beautiful day. We were able to have a bath, with me teaching them how to bathe and splash in the water. I would help them into their clothes that came from the clothesline smelling so fresh. We were able to cuddle for some time in my arms before going off to enjoy a relaxed breakfast.

We had friends to go to the park with or just to play with in our yards, without the worry that today's parents have. Of course, I was a "worry wart" mother and would check on them every so often.

My primary job was to care for my children. I sewed for other people, making quilts and stuffed dolls (like Raggedy Ann) and doll clothes. This kept me from spending much money and allowed me the time with my children.

Many older folks remember "in our days, things were different." Yes, that is true—each generation has their own values, which are made according to events surrounding their lives at that time.

Memories mean different things to different people—my memories of playing with my children and not working outside the home until they were teenagers are just that—MY MEMORIES.

But the ones in this chapter can be shared and enjoyed by all.

This memory is of the weekend before I started working. My friend Rose and I were both starting a full-time job outside the home on Monday. As we are both avid quilters and felt we wouldn't have as much free time to go on material shopping trips, off we went to our favorite local store.

There were several quilts I planned to make that year for gifts and I needed time to pick out just the right colors. One of the quilt patterns was for a Dresden Plate quilt. I needed sixteen colors of rose and wedgewood blue. We stayed in our local store for about three hours with me spending my first month's check!

As time went on we both made time for outings with our other "Saturday girls." Quilting, knitting, cross-stitching, etc. all became a much looked for time away from our jobs outside the home.

My quilts were finished on time that year, but as of this writing, I am far behind with things started but not yet finished. I have my own "fabric and trim" store in my sewing room, but we continue about twice a year to take short trips for something new.

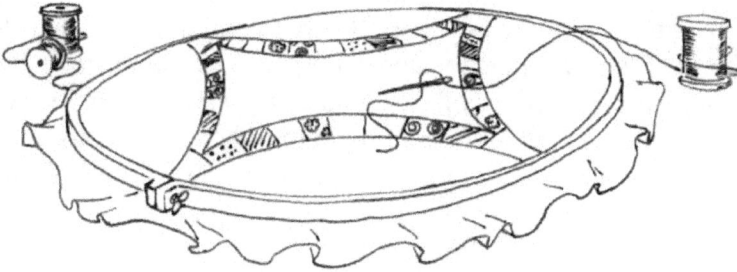

Both Rose and I are still quilters, crafters, etc. Of all the things that we have done over the years, this memory of our fabric shopping trip the weekend before starting our full-time jobs sticks with both of us. We both thought (wrongly) that was the day that we must get fabric because our jobs might interfere with us ever getting fabric again! This brings us much humor each time we relive this memory.

In a childcare setting, one of our duties is to help the children to ask for things politely and to learn some manners. Most parents would like our help in this matter and usually require their child to say, "Yes M'am" or "No, M'am." This is just a task that takes repetition from the child and numerous reminders from us.

This next memory is one that I take great joy in remembering because it reminds me that sometimes we expect too much and other times the children remember more than we do.

When a child asked me one day, "Could you tie my shoe?" I said, "Yes, I will be glad to." And then proceeded to tie his shoe. When I finished, I replied to him, "Thank you for asking me nicely to tie your shoe." He replied, "But I didn't say please." We laughed about this, and I reminded him to say it the next time.

This child was only three years old and had remembered that he needed to use these manners. In my book, he did ask nicely, as he could have just said, "Tie my shoe, now."

It is important to always talk respectfully to children as well as to adults. Children model our behavior and our speech. I use positive words and body language with the children under my care and try very hard to keep the negative out of our classroom. This is hard to do in some circumstances but well worth the effort to THINK BEFORE YOU SPEAK.

❦

One Monday, a parent was very frustrated and nearly at her wits end. Her daughter would not cooperate in getting ready for school, so her mom started bringing her to school half dressed or in her pajamas. The mother would dress or finish dressing her daughter in the hallway, with both crying and screaming. Well, the next day the mother almost threw her in the room half dressed. I said, "Rough morning today?" Mom did not speak. At this point I knew someone was in trouble. We talked about her child not wanting to get dressed. She told me how the child screamed all night and morning, fought to get into the car, and did everything else to make the morning miserable for all.

Well, this single mom needed some relief! I suggested that she get the daughter up when she was ready to walk out the door, bringing her in her pajamas with her clothes and shoes in a bag. She could hand the daughter to me, and I would assist the girl into her day clothes when she was ready. Mom said, "Thank you." The daughter was unhappy on Wednesday and Thursday, but on Friday, it was a different matter. I had told the other parents we were going to have pajama day and all children should come in their pajamas.

Our lesson that day was about what we wear to sleep in and what we did in the morning to prepare for the day. We discussed brushing our teeth, eating breakfast, getting into day clothes, etc. from that day on, the girl's mother had no trouble in the mornings.

Sometimes we need to remember that, as teachers, we must help parents with their day-to-day problems. This is just as important as teaching the children science and math skills.

When I was a staff member at a preschool as a Toddler Teacher, my duties were to give the six children love, guidance, positive discipline, and to teach them some language skills.

Our children in the other classes sang songs at Christmas for their parents. I was not informed when I was hired that I was expected to perform and make my own costume!

Our director wanted to read a story during the program about a tree. This tree was alive and had a speaking part. My first job was to use green net for a Christmas tree costume from head to toe. On this costume, I added red velvet bows, with one at the top of my head hanging down. One of the staff wrapped miniature tree lights around me, and when my turn came, I "proudly" walked down the aisle of the sanctuary with my plug in hand. When I arrived in front, my director plugged me into a wall socket.

I said my part, and was very thankful when the program was over. A strand of 100 miniature lights was rather warm!

Having taught two-year-olds, I feel strongly that the children need to see as many real objects as possible. During the school year, I try to find themes that will keep the children's interest and help them understand the outside world. I have gathered caterpillars for them to watch as they eat, cocoon, and emerge as beautiful butterflies. We have had hamsters, goldfish and even earthworms, which we kept in a pickle jar to see the "roads" that they make.

For several years we had fertile chicken eggs from a local farmer to put in our incubator. Well, this is a fun unit for the children but another one of those projects that keep teachers extremely busy. The eggs need to be turned twice daily. They need a certain amount of water as the days go by and the temperature in the incubator needs to stay at a certain degree. It takes twenty-one days for a regular chicken to hatch. Who turns them on weekends? You guessed it—the teacher! When they do hatch, they need a warm place and food and water to drink. This usually means that we bring out the aquariums (if not in use already, review Chapter 5) and clip-on lamps in addition to old towels. Lots of newspaper is used too to keep clean cages. Chickens really smell up a classroom—more than stinky diapers!

One year, no eggs hatched; they were not fertile. What a shock I had! What would I tell the children? We had been keeping track and they knew that it was the twenty-first day. So, while they were taking their nap, I slipped over to my "chicken man's" house and explained my problem. He quickly gave me an assortment of needed baby chicks. When the children woke up—PRESTO! Baby chickens had hatched. The look on their faces was all that was needed to know that I will continue "hatching" chickens, fertile or not! I just hope my source of eggs and chickens doesn't run out.

We are so busy as young mothers, getting ourselves up and ready for a full day's work, that we yank our children up (sometimes out of a deep sleep), throwing on clothes and send them to school, knowing that they will get something to eat there. Then off to work we go, dreading the end of a day's work, so we can rush to pick up our children at school, head to the grocery store, home to cook dinner, do a few household chores, and send the children to bed, so we can retire to start all over again the next day. That is the routine of today's family! This is a memory of most of our childcare families.

However, along this busy, hectic day are the joys of parenthood that we sometime take for granted. Do you remember thinking of something that would excite your child to move a little faster in the morning—like new shoes to show off to their friends, or maybe to tell of the cookies that they helped you make and eat last night. (Forget about the mess.) These are things that help us get through the morning.

Memories can occur in different places, and all indeed are considered memories.

Do you remember the times you read the same book for weeks before bedtime to your child and then were impressed the night you tried to skip a page or two and you thought your child could read because they caught you?

Even in our hectic busiest days we make memories. Sometimes they are to remind us to take baths at night, laying out everyone's clothes for the next day and to even pack the next day's lunches before going off to bed. Things like this help us to have less hectic mornings.

Today's parents are varied, as I have mentioned before. Some are single parents. This next memory is one of a female child whose father has custody of her.

The young girl was starting her "toilet training" under my care. I noticed that she would stand over the toilet with her pants down, trying to touch herself. I showed her how to sit to "go potty" but she again stood up to try.

It occurred to me that she only watched her father use the toilet and she must have thought that was the way she should use the toilet too. I spoke to her father one afternoon and sure enough, this was what was occurring. Dad did not realize that she was old enough to know what he was doing. We agreed that he could close the bathroom door when he took care of his "potty time."

It is hard for single parents to help their children with certain gender issues. This same situation happens with mothers of sons. We are not all blessed with numerous family members to help us with raising our children and need to look to our childcare teachers or to our social or church families, for the extra assistance needed when situations like the above occur.

Some memories I have are painful to remember. As a professional in childcare, I try to be watchful of children's behavior and notice any health issues.

This is one memory that might have been a tragedy, had I not been observant of a child and had skills in having parent/teacher conferences.

A mother of a child in my care had a two-year-old who would not stay in his bed at night, so she decided to tie him in his bed. We noticed a strange mark around his stomach area when we changed his diaper for several days. When I asked him how he got the marks he said, "Mommy tied me."

When his parents arrived, I sympathized with them but gave them several other ways to help with his nightly problem. One suggestion was to put a gate at his doorway. They tried this and he screamed at first but then settled for the night. The first few nights the child fell asleep on the floor. But as the parents remained consistent and did not remove the gate at night, the child was able to sleep in his own bed without the restraints.

As I explained to the parents, if an emergency arrived, the child might need to move to safety (if, for example, there was a fire in the house) and that he could not do this if he was tied down. This is one of our jobs—to help parents with problems before child abuse occurs. Unfortunately, adults are not given a childcare course before they become parents. We as childcare professionals should always remember to give guidance as needed to these young parents.

⚜

For parents and anyone who works with children, we know that the "Terrific Twos" (also known as the Terrible Twos) are an eye-opener. For those who have not experienced this special time with a two-year-old, borrow one for the weekend.

One year a beautiful, intelligent two-year-old started giving her mother a terrible time. A new baby sister had arrived at their house, and she did not want her there. Her father was in the military and unfortunately for all, had night duty for several months after the baby arrived. Our little girl decided that this was her time alone with Mom and wanted to make sure she received all the attention. For several weeks, when it was time for this two-year-old to go to bed and for Mom to feed the infant, our two-year-old decided to have a temper tantrum. It started off on a small scale. She would throw all her toys on the floors and remove her clothes from the closet, all the while screaming and stomping.

This caused Mom great anxiety. She didn't know what to do and would call Dad to come home to quiet her. Of course, being the loving parent that he was—with a wife in hysterics, a newborn baby and a terrific two-year-old screaming in the background—he raced home right away to settle things before returning back to work.

Well, this behavior of course got worse. Mom said she didn't know

71

what was wrong with her (we did—the baby). So now the two-year-old not only threw her toys and emptied out her closet, but she also emptied out her dresser drawers, pulled the drawers out to the floor, took off her bed linens and even moved the mattress and box springs to the floor.

I asked her mother why she didn't just leave the mess for her child to clean up and why did she call the father to come help. She said she just didn't have the strength to handle her daughter and the infant by herself. Well, we had a talk and I explained that her husband could get sent overseas and she would be by herself with the children then. The thought of being alone with the "terrific" two-year-old seemed to scare her.

I gave her some information on the "Terrific Twos" and suggested that she go about her business the best she could and try to ignore her daughter's temper outburst until it was over (making sure she was safe of course). Then to put her to sleep on the mattress on the floor and tell her she loved her and they would both clean up the mess the next day after preschool. The mother said the girl was too small to pick up her stuff, I quickly explained that she wasn't too small to make the mess in the first place, so she could definitely help pick it up.

A lot of guidance and reassurance from her husband and us helped this family through a crisis in their young lives. The mom felt that she needed help after the newborn arrived and the father had to work at night. The two-year-old felt unwanted and unloved due to the newborn "taking her place," so she did only what in her young little mind she felt she needed to do to get her "rightful" place back. Let us remember that as teachers of young families sometimes we need to help all involved.

Parents sometimes feel guilty about leaving their child with a stranger. If the child cries when the parents leave, some parents feel something is wrong or try to "help the child" by staying longer.

For example, a parent had a hard time leaving her child at school, so she decided to stay until she really had to go to work. At this point, the child said, "Longer, Mommy." So Mom stayed longer to prevent the crying.

This kept up for several weeks, with the child wanting Mom to stay longer each time and the parent getting later and later to work. As I saw the pattern developing, I suggested to the parent to bring a timer, such as a sand hourglass with her. When the sand was gone, Mommy had to go, even if the child cried.

In several days, the child didn't need the hourglass. By the end of the week, the child told her mother at the door, "You can go to work," and then went off to play. What a relief this was to her mom!

For many years our preschool was truly blessed with a staff who worked as a team, were considerate of others, and who stayed together. We had no turnover in staff for several years. During this time, we had staff Christmas parties at someone's home, where the preschool provided the main dish and each staff member brought a side-dish. The staff member whose home we were at provided the drinks (punch, tea, coffee).

We planned special interesting games. We did a "Dirty Santa" game. We watched a video of line dancing and all tried to learn. We laughed with Jeff Foxworthy's redneck jokes on a video, and wore antique hats for amusement.

One year that stands out through the years was the planned "This Is Your Life" for the Pre-K assistant. This wonderful woman had the most remarkable things happen to her. For instance, one day she came to work upset as she realized she gave her dog her birth control pill and took his heartworm pill by mistake. Well we convinced her to call the vet's office for advice. The veterinarian said she was okay, but if she started to bark, to come see him!

For this special Christmas party, we hired a Santa, asked all staff for things our staff "victim" had done over the years, and put together a great "This Is Your Life" book for her. Now we just had to wait for her arrival.

Our Santa was getting hot in his suit and she was still not there. A phone call to the staff member's house revealed that she was too tired to come. After all this planning, we were determined she be there so I spoke to her teenage daughter, told her we had a surprise for her Mom and to get her there soon—Santa was melting. Santa removed some clothes, had a cold drink, and we awaited her arrival, trying to decide if we should put this in her book too.

It was all worth it to see her on Santa's lap as he read "This Is Your Life" to her. We also added another page about how she almost didn't show up for her own party!

Several years ago the State of Florida began requiring that all childcare workers obtain a CDA (refer to Chapter 2). There were five of us who took our CDA course together. At first, we were not really excited about taking this one-year course, but as it was a state requirement that one staff member for every twenty children in a childcare center have one, so we did it. All five of us were lead teachers in five different classrooms.

We left our school on Thursday evenings, attending class at our junior college for three hours a week that year. We sometimes met each other at a fast food restaurant nearby for a quick sandwich for supper before class that evening.

As talented women who had lots of on-the-job training and children of our own, we thought this would be easy. Ha! We had so much information to gather, lesson plans to write (we already did this so it was a breeze) and books on gender and sex to find in regards to the children within our age groups (12 months through five years old). We needed to have a file box to store all this information in and to carry this box to class weekly. At the end of this course, our boxes were quite heavy, and we were grateful we had each other to help with class work on the weekends.

Often we would come in on Friday mornings and talk to our director about the class—how we were not having a lot of fun and how others in the class were reading romance novels or sleeping and not doing their homework. We were quickly reminded that we could be replaced by someone who was eighteen years old with a CDA.

Well, as we griped along the way and kept up with our morning and afternoon teaching jobs and kept up with our A's in class, in addition to our homelife (children, laundry, shopping, cleaning) our center's school board members and our director made plans for us.

When our last class was over, the last evaluations turned in, and we looked forward to having a free Thursday night and a raise in salary, our director sent us an invitation to attend a special celebration on the following Thursday night.

When we arrived, we were asked to put on white graduation caps, and then march in to *Pomp and Circumstance* hummed by our center's board and the director. They congratulated us, told us we would receive pay raises, and told us how proud of us they were. This has been a great memory for me.

Parents try to be the best they can for their child, but forget that they need to care for themselves too. This memory is one I have used with other parents who forget to meet their own needs too.

A young mother whose husband worked at night was always tired and saying she had no time to herself. She would pick up her child right after work (3 p.m.) and go to the grocery store, and then home to unload, put away groceries and cook supper.

Her child was always hungry and didn't want to behave in the store. He was ready for some movement, as he had just woken from an hour and a half nap when she got him from school. One day I suggested that she purchase her groceries, go home, put them away, and start supper before coming to pick up her son from school. She said she would feel guilty doing that. I reminded her that she paid tuition for the whole day, so she should try it once.

The next week she gave it a try, she even had the food on the table. Well needless to say, this worked very well for her. In a few weeks, she informed us that she would be picking her child up almost at closing time, as she was going to go to the gym to work out. Things became a lot easier for her now and her child could work off some energy before going home.

Was she neglecting her child by letting him stay a bit longer at childcare? I think not. Isn't it a great service to do for our parents? Yes, we like it when parents keep their child at home when they do not have to go to work. This gives us one less child in our classroom. But when do the parents have time for themselves without the children? For the parents to be the best they can be to themselves, their job, and most especially to their loved ones, they must have that little bit of time for themselves too.

One of our playgrounds borders two walls on another building, becoming a great place for weeds to grow. In the warm weather, roly polys are abundant in the weeds. The children of all ages become excited when they find one, which usually leads to finding a half a dozen or so by the end of the day. These small bugs tickle the children's hands as then crawl with their numerous legs. Sometimes the bugs curl up like a ball, hence their name.

One morning a two-year-old was having fun watching them curl and uncurl in his hand. He came to me after a few minutes of play, telling me that he had one up his nose. I was very surprised that he would put it up there, but sure enough, he had. I called his parents to come look at it, as according to licensing requirements we are not allowed to pull anything out of noses, ears, or even to remove splinters from fingers. The boy's father came and took him to the car where he proceeded to pull out the roly poly.

For some time, I did not allow the children to play with these bugs. This is a memory that reminds me when children are quiet, we need to check on them, even when they appear to be having fun.

In a childcare setting it is sometimes hard for children not to be able to do things that are "normal" for them to do at home. We need to be very careful not to show any displeasure we might have with the way a parent raises their child, especially in front of the child.

This next memory is one of those times.

While on the playground, one day with my two-year-old class, I noticed one of the boys urinating on a bush. I explained to him that we used the toilet inside and not the bush. He told me that he and his dad use the bushes all the time at their house. (This child had turned three years old and was quite vocal.) When the child's father came to pick him up, I asked him to talk to his son about this matter. The father told me that boys do these things and that it was natural. I admitted it is natural for the male population to urinate outside, however we could not at school. I reminded him that if he had a little girl, who had seen his son's privates, that he would not be happy with me for allowing the boys to urinate outside.

The father reminded me that it is a male thing again and then pulled out a $50.00 bill. He gave it to me saying his son would like his friends to get Burger King meals the next day for lunch. Of course, I continued to urge his son to use the toilet and remind him that he could only urinate outside with his dad.

The children were excited about having french fries for lunch the next day, and the parents were excited that they did not have to fix their child a lunch. I, however, have a memory that stays with me—that I need to watch the boys each year, as they try to do the same thing.

When both teachers and parents work together, giving children life experiences, the bond for the child is enriched. I choose a theme each month for my two-year-old class. The theme includes a color and shape for the month. Language development, gross motor skills, group time, finger plays and songs. On Fridays we have Show and Tell, where the children can bring something from home to show their friends which goes with our theme. This helps their social skills and their language development.

One month my theme was "The Farm." For Show and Tell, one of the children's grandmothers asked if she could bring a chicken. At the time I was a teacher and not the director, so I spoke to our director who said she could as long as it was not set loose somewhere. (Please remember to always check with the director, as she or he knows the rules and regulations of what is allowed by licensing requirements and the health regulations.)

The chicken named Matilda was truly the best Show and Tell item that I have ever had. (The python snake was not nearly as good.) Matilda was found in the garage by the grandmother. When plants were brought in for the winter, apparently Matilda took roost in a hanging plant. When the grandmother began feeding her, she became a pet, following her around whenever she went in the yard.

The child and the grandmother brought Matilda to school in a covered cage with plenty of food and water. When the grandmother sat in chair in the middle of the classroom with eighteen two-year-olds around, the fun really began! The child fed Matilda live crickets from her own little hand, and we all watched Matilda eat them. The children enjoyed watching and seeing some of the crickets escape into our room. They heard the purring noise that Matilda made when the grandmother smoothed down her feathers with her hand.

What a learning experience we all had that day!

When I was an assistant to the director, one of the most important aspects of the job was to assist the other teachers with any and all problems that arise. This may mean to fix a leaking toilet, fix the gate when a child runs into it with a bike, assist the infant room with several crying babies, or help a child find his "listening ears."

One of the Pre-K children had a "listening ears" problem. I would spend time with him to find out why he would not listen when his teacher spoke to him. Sometimes he would have to come to my two-year-old classroom as he had lost his classroom privilege. This had been agreed upon with his parent. They too were unsure what to do to help him. We knew that a method had to be established for when he acted up at school.

On one particular week this little four-year-old was with me more than he was in his own classroom. He would play with the two-year-olds on the playground, missing his own playground time. He ate lunch with my children, not his peers. Sometimes he had to take a nap with my children, in lieu of his own classroom. This all depended on what time of day his "listening ears" clogged up.

When he was with the two-year-old children, this young man was not happy. He would ask every few minutes if he could go back to his class and I would reply, "I am sorry but you were kicked out of your class today. You must stay with me now."

The following week, this young man did not come to see me. I was puzzled as to why—did he finally find his "listening ears" or was he not at school this week? I finally asked his teacher how he was. She replied that indeed he was there and that he even said a prayer about me that day. I asked her what and why. She said that he started misbehaving and that she told him if he did it one more time he would have to go see me.

This smart little boy got down on his knees and folded his hands and said, "Please, God, don't send me to Miss Peggy." We were all surprised, and knew then he was trying to get help for his misbehavior.

It was almost a month before I was asked to come help this young man find his "listening ears."

Children do not intentionally act up. They are sometimes just checking out the situation to see what they can get away with and what they can't. Children need guidance along the way at every age and stage. Sometimes in a childcare setting we get frustrated and are not sure of the correct method to handle some situations. I have always found that keeping communication with the child's parents open is a big help. Since they are the child's first teachers, they usually can help you decide what works and what doesn't.

A child in my care for two years was soon leaving our center. He had an older brother who attended another school for after-school care. Our center was not large enough to have this program. Unfortunately we often lost a younger child due to this situation.

My young friend told us he was going to a new school at the airport. I explained that the airport doesn't have any schools for boys and girls, but he was very insistent. As this school is in my neighborhood and I knew the owner, I understood why he thought he was going to school at the "airport."

We live in Pensacola, Florida. It is a wonderful town and home to the

Blue Angels. The owner of the preschool for many years had named her center Blue Angel Early Learning Center. It is close to the back gate of the Navy base and the road intersects at Blue Angel Highway. She has a small airplane in the Blue Angels' colors with Blue Angels written on it. Knowing all of this, I tried to explain to my young friend that it was not the airport but just an airplane to go along with their school name.

Later in the day, I asked the young boy if I could leave our school and teach at his new school. He replied, "No." When I asked him why, he told me, "Because you said I wasn't going to school at the airport."

I guess I didn't explain very well that his school wasn't the airport. What would you think?

Our CDA certification needed to be renewed and the class four of us chose was a High Scope class. Once again, we left work and went to school for three hours once a week.

The High Scope class was a different approach to teaching. We gained lots of knowledge, had debates with the instructor as to "our way" versus hers, and were able to maintain our perfect A's and renew our CDA for another five years.

One of our assignments was to make a classroom complete with furniture, people, etc. Now, this classroom was in miniature form, about the size of a box that holds twenty-four cans of soda. It also needed to be arranged as we learned in class. As employees of a well-known childcare center, we wanted ours to be THE BEST!

I went to the local cake shop and bought plastic dolls and cribs. We cut pictures from magazines and wallpaper books. We made miniature bookshelves, blocks, tables, chairs, diaper stackers, and toilets. Our outside playground had swings, slides, sandboxes, balls, sand, grass and concrete. We painted our walls, and had carpet and tile floors too!

We spent weeks on this project. We were very excited to see each other's. What fun we had! We took great pleasure in showing ours off to anyone we could grab, especially our center's board members who we wanted to make sure knew we were indeed the valued employees we thought we were.

❉

The first childcare center I worked for was blessed to have a maintenance man. Not all centers have one. I have so many memories of Mr. Bob that I would like to share some of them with you.

My first encounter with Mr. Bob was one morning when I arrived in my classroom to find a red rose in a vase. I thought, how special of someone! Mr. Bob was exactly that—SPECIAL—to all of us! He would continue to surprise us with a flower from time to time. One in a vase for every classroom.

❉

Mr. Bob loved any type of party. He would arrive at the center sometimes about 1:30 p.m., somehow knowing we had a birthday cake or cupcakes for snack that afternoon. The first thing he would say was, "Hey, Peg, do you have any birthdays today?"

❉

My toddlers loved the sandbox in the afternoons. The sun was too hot in the morning for them to play in it. Mr. Bob made sure the little ones had sand to play in that was free of any weeds. He was always pulling out weeds and making sure no "sticker vines" grew along the sides. I never had to worry about ants as every weekend he checked for any that might hide.

❉

When Mr. Bob's granddaughter came into my room, it was not surprising to find him sitting in the sandbox playing with the children.

82

What fun to see him laughing and digging with her! She didn't care for sand on her hands but she loved her Opa (German for grandfather).

For a few years, the center had an activity day outside. We called this our field day. Each classroom provided an activity for children aged two to five. The parents from each classroom volunteered to help the children with the activity, while teachers took small groups around to each table. The activities included stringing noodles for a necklace, using markers on a sun visor, going fishing, and visiting a duck pond. We had pony rides, puppet making, a lemonade stand, icing and eating sugar cookies and something to bounce in. Mr. Bob loved those days! It was one day he didn't mind getting up early or missing a game of golf. He would check the riding lawn mower and the small wagon he pulled behind it about a week before this event. He gave the children a ride around the parking lot, three or four at a time. What fun they had with him! A teacher was either in the wagon with the children or walking alongside it for safety. My first ride was with my group of toddlers.

When we had staff meetings or workshops at night, Mr. Bob was always in the parking lot watching our cars as security. He made sure we made it safely to our cars when the meeting was over. It was always a pleasure to have him help us at night. We never worried about being alone.

On Mr. Bob's 70th birthday, his family had a surprise party for him and invited some of the staff that had been at the center for a long time. I felt so proud to go to this party! Mr. Bob had done so much for the center and for me. His children and family had hot dogs, hamburgers, and all the trimmings. The cake was beautiful as well as delicious. The family had worked hard to make this a special day for him.

Once, I wanted a low shelf in my classroom for the two-year-old children. I wanted to put a fish tank on this shelf for the children to look at. As I had several children with emotional problems, I felt that watching fish would help them calm down when things didn't go their way. Mr. Bob was very happy to help with this. He put a long shelf across the wall with spindle legs and even glued tile on the top. What fun the children had sitting in chairs or just standing, watching the fish. We even used this for watching other live critters.

Many memories of Mr. Bob fill my heart, as he was such a part of the center. Mr. Bob went into semi-retirement when he started having some health problems. He would come around to visit us whenever possible. The day Mr. Bob passed away was a very sad one. The things that he had done at the center to make the staff's life easier can still be seen. His handyman skills outshone those of most people. Some things, it was a mystery how he repaired them.

Mr. Bob's grandson was later in my Pre-K class. At times I could see that little twinkle that his Opa had. I am positive that Mr. Bob is watching over us from above. There are days when something goes wrong and I reach for the silver duck tape—I know that Mr. Bob is leading me to another mystery repair job!

One nice sunny day, our three-year-olds were outside playing. They had been playing for about 30 minutes when one child came up to his teacher and bit her on the bottom. Yes, you read that right. A three-year-old bit his teacher's bottom!

The teacher turned around, a little startled, and asked the child, "Did you just bite my bottom?" The child replied, "Yes." The teacher looked very puzzled at this young three-year-old under her care and asked him,

"Why?" The child then replied, "Because I am a cute little spider."

We didn't think it was "cute" for a spider or a child to do. I was put to the task of finding a meaningful way of disciplining him. The child watched the Spiderman movie and was trying to do things from the movie all week. For instance, he tried to "make webs" and "fly" from one piece of playground equipment to another. The child was wearing a Spiderman shirt that day, so I chose to replace his shirt. I told him that Spiderman had to go home as we do not bite a teacher's or anyone else's bottoms or body parts. We would like him to be himself today as he had better behavior than Spiderman. He said, "Okay."

It is amazing what children can pick up at the movies! I saw the movie and did not see Spiderman bite anyone's body—guess I fell asleep during that part.

Many years ago a training class I attended had a puppet to use daily along with a lesson plan book, classroom rules, and songs. This workshop was from the Peace Education Foundation. Our puppet for interaction was a furry cat called I-Care-Cat. I was excited to use this puppet along with all the new information, as my classroom that year held sixteen children—eleven of whom were boys. Boy, did I need some "positive discipline" tools!

On Monday, I took this valuable information and the cat puppet to school all prepared—Ha! Ha! Ha! Little did I know that my children wanted to know where his toys were, his blanket for naptime and even his car seat, since he came to school in my car.

Needless to say the next day, the I-Care-Cat had a car seat (a doll's), a stuffed mouse and ball of yarn to play with, and a blanket for naptime. (Remember the collections of stuff I have?)

I-Care-Cat has helped me in lessons of learning each other's names, how we don't wipe our noses with our "paws," and how we put our "paws" over our mouths when we cough. This valuable puppet and the lessons have helped me tremendously in directing children's behavior, in modeling positive behavior with my friends and co-workers. In the first month, my classroom atmosphere changed.

I have been so impressed that I started sharing this information with our parents and other staff at workshops. The parents use the I-Care-Cat in the workshops, sing some of his songs, and learn other methods to get positive results with their children.

I have included the address and phone number below for you, should you be interested in a great tool for your classroom.

Peace Education Foundation
1900 Biscayne Boulevard
Miami, Florida 33131-1025
http://www.peace-ed.org/

When I first started teaching, I became a one-year-old teacher, and then moved to the class of two-year-olds. I thought that nothing was any better than being a teacher of the "Terrific Twos."

As two-year-olds are closer to the ground than adults are, I found myself on the floor most of my day. The older I became, the more my legs didn't want to move the way two-year-old children do. Our Pre-K teacher was going to retire at the end of the school year, so I wrote a letter to our Board of Directors asking that I be considered for her position. I was not sure that this move was going to be as rewarding as the position with the two-year-olds.

The two-year-olds and the Pre-K children have many things in common. Each child wants to be the star of the class, and wants to make sure that they have their fair share of attention from the teacher, and they both throw temper tantrums from time to time. The Pre-K children's tantrums are not as frequent as the twos are.

After a few months, I felt that I have missed out by not being a Pre-K teacher before. The twos did need me, and I was rewarded with lots of hugs, and the knowledge that I helped them increase their language and motor skills, among others, but something about the Pre-K children stole my heart.

The lesson is that you never know what is on the other side of the playground. I want to recommend to you that if one age doesn't suit you, then change to another age group. Children of all ages need someone who cares for them, has patience, and can give them things needed while their parents are away.

This is a memory of when I changed classrooms. I was going to be a Pre-K teacher. This was a time of uncertainty on my part, as I had not been one before and was unsure that I could be the best that I needed to be in this position.

I had watched other teachers of this classroom change the room around to suit their particular teaching style and knew what was in the classroom. I am a hands-on teacher and feel that the children under my care learn best by experiencing things that way too.

Now, how to set up the classroom according to my teaching methods became a problem for me. The classroom was small but could be made cozy. I knew I wanted a science table, a library corner, an art table, a block center, a home living center and a station with hands-on work materials. Now where in the world would all this go in a small room?

The quilter in me decided to get graph paper and map out my new classroom. Once everything was on paper, I went about trying to put things in place. This required me to stay late and to work on Saturday, both of which I enjoyed as I love to see the pieces come together.

This particular classroom didn't have all the necessary things I felt it needed. I began moving things from my garage into the new classroom. This made my husband extremely happy, as now we could maybe have a garage instead of a storage unit!

My move into this room was very noticeable. Everyone wondered where in the world all my "junk" was going. I am happy to say that it all fit exactly where I graphed it. I have a number of items in my room that I possibly could get by without, but what fun the children and I have using them.

After about six months in that room, my anxiety lessened. I still hoped that I was the best that I could be for these young children. It is not how much stuff you have, but how much time, energy, and love you are willing to give on a daily basis. I think I have lots to share with them.

One day at lunch, one of my Pre-K students told the following story. I hope you find lots of interesting tidbits in his story, as I did.

"One time my parents went to a fancy dinner and I went outside all dressed as an ogre with my sword, snake, and dog. A bad guy, like a swordsman was there and I kicked his butt, stabbed him with my sword. My snake and dog bit his head off and ate him up—all gone—and then my dog and snake died. You know what—my picture was in the newspaper with my dog and snake and the big fat bad guy too! When I roped him I stuck the sword in him. My parents were getting their dessert. When they came home I was on the roof with the helmet on, with a whole bunch more of bad guys."

At this point I asked him, "Didn't you get into trouble for opening the door when your parents were gone?" He then said, "I didn't get into trouble because I was so good kicking their butt. My parents had some fantastic news—they were giving me a motorcycle." Then he said to me, "ISN'T THAT THE BEST STORY YOU HAVE EVER HEARD?"

I could not believe that I had just heard it myself, so I went to my room to get some paper and a pencil and asked him to tell it to me again. I wrote it as he told it. Honestly, this is all from a Pre-K child!

The children in our Pre-K class sleep on mats during naptime. I usually put out the mats as the children are going to wash their hands for lunch. Several of the boys like to make a running jump onto their mats, causing the mats to move a little. This looked fun, but to me it was a safety issue. I asked the boys not to do this, as they might get hurt. One of them kept on after I had asked them not to do this more than once, and then I firmly talked with him when he almost hit his head on the table.

I asked him in my not-so-nice tone of voice why he was still jumping on his mat. I then said that if he continued he could sleep on the hard, cold, dirty floor instead of the soft mat. As I was talking to him, one of my other Pre-K boys said, "Ohh, Miss Peggy is really pissed off now!" I was really shocked at this. I turned around to him and said, "Excuse me, the day that I am those words is the day I need to find another job!"

Children overhear what adults say more than we realize. We must always guard our language when they are around. I do not know where he learned those words, but I have tried not to use that same tone of voice again.

One day I was discussing mammals with the children. We were learning what a mammal is and where they live. We used our K-W-L chart (what we Know, what we Want to know, and what we Learned) as the children came up with questions.

One of the boys wanted to know which mammal was the fastest. My answer disturbed him greatly. He said his Dad told him the jaguar was the fastest and I had said that the cheetah was. The center did not have Internet service, so I said I would check on my computer later.

The next day, he was still not happy. My paper still said the cheetah was the fastest long-distance, and the jaguar was the fasted short-distance. This still wasn't correct to him "cause my Dad is always right."

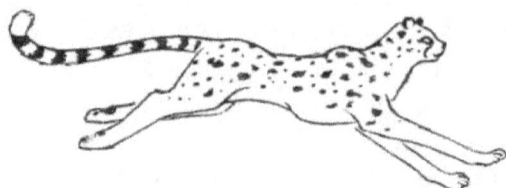

For this math lesson, we lined up outside together and had two markers—one shorter than the other. The one who got to the shortest first was the jaguar and the one who got to the longest first was the cheetah.

I had been sick with the latest bug and was unable to "run the race" until after Christmas. So during the holiday break, I tried to get into "cheetah" shape so that this lesson would turn out in my favor. Isn't hands-on learning great?

During one November, I was working on lesson plans for my December Pre-K class. I remembered our affiliated-church had recently adopted a family for the holidays. When I found out that one of the children in the family was four years old, my decision was made. Wouldn't it be nice for my Pre-K class to purchase all her Christmas items and learn the true meaning of the holidays?

My next step was to find out what the child needed and to approach my co-workers and director with this idea. The guidelines from the sponsoring agency were that the child in the family would have eight presents to unwrap, consisting of four items of clothing and four toys.

During circle time, I approached the class with the idea and they said sure. I pulled out our K-W-L chart and off we went. We KNEW our "angel" was a girl and she was four years old, like them, "What would she like?" was my next question for them. As they said things, my co-worker checked the items on her list. One of our boys said, "New underwear." When I said, "New underwear?" he replied, "Yes, new underwear feels good!"

The discussion led to how are we going to buy things—none of us had any money and the teachers were the only ones with a job. Some thought we could charge it (no one had a charge card). Some thought they could ask their parents, but I reminded them it was our job as we agreed to do this for our angel girl. What great joy came to me with the next answer, from two children at the same time, "We can cook and sell our stuff!" This was what I wanted them to do—how great that they came up with the answer by themselves!

I introduced a letter a week and we cooked something with that letter. We had become quite good chefs and had a recipe book started.

Now for a discussion on what to cook—the ideas ranged from pizza to French toast to muffins. We took a vote (math lesson) and muffins won. We went back to our K-W-L chart and decided we wanted to know the kinds of muffins people liked.

We asked the parents and the other staff what were their favorites. Our list became blueberry, lemon poppy seed, banana nut, cranberry orange and cinnamon streusel. I purchased the ingredients for the children, and we discussed the receipt (language lesson). I then placed the receipt in the jar, and off we went to cook our muffins (science lesson).

Next we needed to know how much to charge. Some of the children's conversation on this follows:

Teacher:    "How much should we charge?"
Child:       "One dollar."
Teacher:    "A dollar each? Isn't that too much?"
Child:       "No, it's hard work to make them."
Teacher:    "What about two for a dollar?"
Child:       "No way, that would be two dollars?"

We finally agreed at $0.75 each.

Then we had discussions on where and how to sell them. It was decided to use a table and chair by the director's office. Some children came early and put on a baker's hat, apron, and a nametag to sell the muffins between 6:30 a.m. and 8:30 a.m., when the largest group of parents arrive. During the day other children would sell to staff, and to a group of quilting ladies who visited the connecting building on Thursday.

My next question to them was, "How will we get people to buy the muffins?" The children said, "We can ask them." "We can make signs." "Yes, like a stop sign—buy here!" (problem-solving skills). So out came the poster board, glitter, glue, silk flowers, buttons, beads, bows and markers.

We posted our signs on doors and had our table and chairs ready along with a money jar. The muffins were wrapped in zip-lock bags and placed in pretty baskets with a cloth liner from our home-living center.

The next week, we made Chex party mix and repeated this process as we needed "millions of dollars" to purchase our angel girl her presents.

On Monday, I laid out our dollars and we counted out what the children owed me for ingredients and the presents, including wrapping paper (math lesson).

The children asked me if I would buy them a tea set, for our home living section, and a baby doll that came with books and makeup, because it was "so cute." I reminded them that we had lots of stuff in our room and that the holidays were a special time for giving things to others.

We discussed how our angel girl was going to feel and how we felt about giving to others. They answered with comments like, "warm," "great," "what we should do," "happy," "let's do it again," and "yeah, we can buy more people stuff."

The day came and off went the gifts. Our giving was done for now. But more giving of our hearts followed over the next few months.

In January, the children were still talking about giving to others. Someone brought a coat to share with someone who needed one and some brought in mittens to share with their friends when we went outside to play. This lesson was shared by all eleven children and their families and continues to bring happiness to others.

❧

While eating McDonald's chicken nuggets one day (all children and staff), I was sitting at the head of the table with children on both sides. A child on my right said, "Look, Ms. Peggy. The moon!" I turned my head to see what was there, and this little fellow reached over, grabbed one of my nuggets, and put it in his mouth. He then told me, "Oh, you missed it!"

❧

A two-year-old came in one morning and said, "My mom was fighting with a man in the bed last night." Well, we were afraid someone had broken into her house or something. When her mother came to pick up the child, I asked if she was okay. She was puzzled and asked why. I explained what her child had told us. She started laughing—it was her brother she was "fighting" with. He had a picture of her when she was a baby, naked on a bearskin rug and was going to show it to others. She explained that she was trying to get it away from him at the time her daughter came in to the room. Boy, were we relieved! Children do say the craziest things!

❧

While on the playground, a four-year-old child approached her teacher and said "You are going to be a grandma." The teacher replied, "Why do you say that?" The child replied, "Because you have crinkles on your neck."

❧

Once, when discussing a child's bedtime routine with the child's grandmother, I found out the child was not going to bed until 10 p.m. I replied that no wonder he was tired in the morning and that maybe he should go to bed about 8 p.m. The grandmother looked at her grandson and said, "Did you hear that?" The child replied, "You need to quit talking to Ms. Peggy."

One of the traits that Pre-K children have is their language. At this age, they have a language explosion. One Friday I decided to write down a few of the things that my Pre-K children said during the day:

1. "Good job, son." (One child said to another who was pretending to wash the floor.)

2. "I'll give you $3.00 for that $10.00 bill." (One child to another while playing with the toy cash register.)

3. "Can someone baby-sit my baby? I need to do my writing." (One child's request when the classes' writing paper was placed on the table.)

4. "If you don't do that to me again, I won't tell the teacher." (One child to another. Wow, what problem-solving skills, and the child didn't do it again.)

5. "Ms. Peggy, here is a plastic bag. We aren't allowed to have this in our kitchen center." (Bag found by a child after a parent dropped it.)

6. "This store is about to close. I have to put the money up. You have five more minutes and then I have to drive home." (Playing in the dramatic play center.)

7. While looking at a map of the state of Florida, with a notebook and a pencil in hand, two children were discussing how to get somewhere, "Let's go to the river first. Okay, now let's see, go around this place, now into the forest. It will take a long time. Am I going the right

way?" The children were looking at different places along the map then went around the room and back to check the map again. This went on for twenty minutes until they finally arrived at the library center and one read a book to the other.

When one of my Pre-K children wet his pants, I asked him, "Why didn't you tell me you needed to go potty?" He replied, "Why didn't you call me to go potty first?"

While telling her grown daughter who stopped by to visit, "Bye. I will miss you, and I love you" a child in the teachers' care asked, "Does that mean you don't love *us* anymore?"

A father said, "You know they are growing-up when they go to bed in their own bed and then wake up in the middle of the night, they come to you."

"My butt itches, they should have made your butt in the front and your tally-whacker in the back."

"I can't take a bubble baths anymore because I farted."

# ·ﻭﻝ Chapter 8 ﻝﻉﻭ
## Becoming an Owner

As I mentioned in previous chapters, I was employed for one childcare center for nearly 15 years before deciding to open my own. While I had thought about this for years, the change was prompted by the childcare center that I worked for deciding to close for a time period so that they could build a larger structure.

At the time, I was the Director and tried to assist the building committee in locating a temporary building for us between moving from our location to another location that would take some time to build. However, Hurricane Ivan had damaged many buildings and none were suitable for our purpose. We found small places, but we had almost 80 children to move. Some of the spaces that we looked at did not meet licensing standards either. It was an extremely sad day when the center decided there was no choice, for various reasons, but to close until a new facility could be built. What sadness—the school had been open for almost 25 years and was well-known in our town.

It was decided that the last day of school would be Friday, February 3, 2006. As the Director, my responsibility was to box-up all the materials and make an inventory list for storage. When we started taking down things, it became more apparent that this was real. Ms. Vicki wrote the following message on the wall of the infant room: *"Laughter, love, joy, tears, friendship and so much more shared over the last 13 ½ years in this room. Memories will last me forever long after these walls are torn down. I thank God for all the friends I have made and people who have touched my life. Most of all I am thankful for all the joy I have had with my babies. As the last day draws near, tears will be shed but I will treasure every day I had in this room. I do wish things could have turned out differently but it will be okay in the end. Thanks for all the memories."* These words expressed what was in most of our thoughts and hearts!!!

Now what would I do? I needed and wanted a job, and children needed a place to go. I could not think about doing anything else except work with children. Since I was getting older, I wasn't sure if anyone would hire me. I had worked up to vacation time, paid personal days off, and holidays. Now I would start at the beginning again. The emotions ranged from sadness to frustration to anger.

During the Christmas holidays of 2005, I talked about the details with my family. My son, daughter-in-law, and daughter thought it was time for us to venture out on our own. Between all of us, we had degrees in business, psychology, marketing, and twenty years of classroom experiences with all ages of children, and a Director/Owner Credential. Mike and Diane, my son and daughter-in law, decided that they would purchase a building for a childcare center and make all the business decisions necessary.

I knew of a building for sale as I had taken training there in October. It was a cute building, and the owner was someone I had worked with over the years. Mike and Diane met with her, and soon the building became ours. This building was a childcare center in the late 1940s, early 1950s called "Wee Wisdom." Things were coming together fast for us!

The building seemed perfect for us, from the size to the screened in porch to a gazebo in the front. However, it is located between two well-established schools and off the main road. We felt a small preschool was what we wanted. In this way, we could know our children and families, they were not just numbers. A lot of advertisement would be needed, but hopefully my reputation in the community would help us get started along with the children we might bring with us from the other school.

The first thing we did was to meet with a representative from the Department of Children and Families, the State of Florida Health Department and the Fire Inspector to see what must be done to open, in just the 30 days that we had until the other school closed. Fortunately our newly purchased building had been a childcare center before, and most everything was up-to-code and up-to-date. However we needed to replace a fence, and put in an additional sink in the kitchen/office area, and a mop sink had to be installed outside which required a licensed plumber. The sink is to be used for disposing of mop water and any other liquids. The expense for the mop sink was nearly $600.00. Wow, we didn't figure on that expense!

At this point, I decided to tell the center that I was venturing out on my own and starting my own childcare center. This was hard to do—I still am not sure how I felt at that moment. I never thought I would leave the school much less be the Director of a family-owned business. Would they accept what I was doing and allow me to advertise to our existing parents and staff? I had hoped that maybe they would be relieved to some extent—they too were upset about closing and what would happen to our families and staff. I felt that the parents would not be pressured to find a place for their child right away and that we could offer some of the staff employment, which would relieve them of that pressure over the Christmas holidays. It turned out that my concerns were unwarranted, and they wished me the best.

A preschool needs teachers with a CDA or higher degree (remember Chapter 2). I tried to obtain the best staff we could afford, and those who would create a positive atmosphere in their classrooms. Sadly, I could not take all the staff from one school to another nor all of the children because we would be a smaller school. Our new school had room for only four classrooms, so we decided not to take infants (they could come to us when they were one-year-old). We had some children who didn't come with us due to our location as it wasn't close enough for them to make the drive. We brought twenty-one children with us and became completely full the first week that we were open.

All during this 30 day window that we had before we opened, we needed to come up with a Parent and Staff Handbook, enrollment forms, hours of operation, a holiday schedule, tuition prices, staffing, find a payroll company, open a bank account, purchase insurance, create a corporation, make a website and of course, a name for our school! A sign for the building, business cards, and phone number were all needed too! Many names for the childcare center were tossed around. I remember Sharon taking Montessori classes at the building we bought back when it was still a childcare center. She was a teacher with us in the morning, and in the afternoon she went to class. She always stated,

"I have to go to Jamison now." Jamison was the name of the street where the school is located. This stuck with me and I could think of no other name than Jamison Street Preschool. We all agreed with this and since we needed numerous advertisement methods, it was easy for someone to find our location.

The inside of the building was clean, however I wanted a different color for the inside of the building. Sharon suggested a subtle grey. We knew if it wasn't painted before we moved in, it probably would not get done. What a challenge we had before us—we worked our eight to ten hour jobs at our old school and worked nights and weekends at Jamison. I came during lunch breaks to meet the plumber and take needed supplies. Sharon, Vicki (our Pre-K teachers) and their families along with my family and friends all helped to paint all the walls, clean windows, measure and put up blinds, stack paper products, clean toilets etc. Sharon's husband, Larry, made a few shelves and chairs.

A loft was in our kitchen/office area, so Larry rebuilt it in another classroom. Our family members and friends who did not paint or remodel took the bulk supplies of plastic spoons and napkins and sorted them into individual bags for each day's use. So many people came out to give us their well-wishes. The neighbors welcomed us saying it was good to hear children's laughter again. As we are licensed for forty-five children, we were glad the neighbors sent their approval.

During this time of Saturday and Sunday workdays for nearly five weeks, several family members and friends dropped by with lunch. It was so rewarding to know that we not only had our family and friends support us but parents of the children as well. Several parents came to help paint or clean the playground. One father volunteered to clean the leaves and trim the trees from the playground. We had a tree growing in the middle of the monkey bars. He also found someone who could take down the old chain-linked fence over the holidays and replace it with the taller one that we needed.

We needed a refrigerator for the school. This was to keep all our snacks that I furnished. As a small school, we do not have a formal kitchen. Only a counter with two sinks, a microwave and the refrigerator, along with cabinets to place non-perishable snacks in. We went to look for a refrigerator, measuring the space we had before we went. It was very funny the Saturday they delivered it. The refrigerator was too big to come through the door, so the delivery men tried to take the door off the hinges but could not. Finally they removed the doors to the refrigerator and brought it in. Unfortunately they broke one of the door handles and had to bring us a new one.

I closed the center where I had worked for so long on February 3, 2006 and opened Jamison Street Preschool on February 6, 2006. This would not have been possible without the support from all licensing agents and family and friends. The weekend was spent finishing up the last minute things, making sure that our paperwork was ready. (Parents had filled-out enrollment forms and signed papers the week before as well as staff employment information.) Were the sign-in sheets ready for each class, did the children have names on their cubbies (so parents knew where to put lunches, clothes etc.), did we have enough staff coverage for the day, were the correct number of chairs and cots available for all children, did we have toilet paper, soap dispensers, playground equipment for play and did we have lesson plans for all ages for the day? These were things we double-checked. How little did I realize that my duties over the years at the other school had prepared me for the challenges at Jamison!!

The day arrived and all staff came to work and all children attended. The local TV news came to do a quick interview and numerous family and friends sent flowers, balloons and good wishes. Even the previous owner brought us flowers and sincere wishes. Mike and Diane attended opening day too. What a surprise we had when we realized that we needed a gate at the entrance to the toddler bathroom. One of the one-year-olds went to "play in the potty water." Mike ran off to the nearest store to get this item we had overlooked.

Over the next few years we have had numerous ups and downs as most childcare centers do. We have constant need of hiring and advertising for more children to fill empty spots. This is part of the nature of the childcare industry. The need for new work materials, an additional fence, a punch-coded lock for the front door along with numerous other items lead us to find fundraising ideas. As I mentioned in another chapter, payroll is the largest expense that a childcare center has. But in order to provide the quality care that is needed, a staff member should make more than minimum wage. At the same time, the only money we have coming in is the weekly tuitions. This must cover all our costs.

One of our challenges was to keep the lock on the front gate (the gate to the parking lot) locked. Even with a sign "keep gate locked," our parents sometimes left it wide open. The front of the school has a playground on one side. When the children see their parents drive up, it is normal behavior for a four-year-old to go running to them. If the gate is open or unlocked, then the children can run to the parking lot, which gave me a few grey hairs. We invested $500.00 to put up a short wood fence by the playground area with two locks on it. The children can see over it but cannot climb over it. This gave us assurance that we would not lose anyone.

We purchased a punch-coded lock for our front door with one of our first fundraisers. Mike found one on the internet and we had a handyman to install it for several hundred dollars. Wow, this worked great! We gave the code to the parents and staff. Now no one could come into the building unless they had the code. This was another way that we could keep the children safe, as well as the staff.

Several sad occurrences happened over the early years. The husband of one of our staff suddenly passed away. This was a special couple. They were blessed with two children and three grandchildren. They had been together since high school. He was close to retirement and they were going on their first cruise to Alaska two weeks before his sudden death. This happened after only two years of opening Jamison. As tragic as this was for all of us, I felt that we were blessed to all be together, in lieu of each of us working in different areas of town. We were able to be a comfort to our friend and surround her with passion and guidance in her time of sorrow. Within a few months another staff member passed away suddenly due to health issues. We were once again comforted by each other and by our parents. Jamison is a small center, it has heart and soul, we are family to each other only by the fact that we work with each other. We have our disagreements; however as a "family" we work things out. Life gives us ups and downs throughout our lifetime, but we can learn to cope by having close family and friends and the parents' support during these times.

When you have your own business (family or otherwise), everything that happens is a reflection of you. As a new business in this challenging profession, a work week for me consists of 60-70 hours along with an occasional Saturday work day. We do not have the extra funds for a cleaning company so we all clean—sometimes on Saturday. The maintenance men are usually us. I can hit a nail straight, measure correctly for blinds or furniture, change light bulbs, have fallen in love with certain cleaners, and know how to grab a dad or my husband when something heavy needs lifting.

A child gave me a wind chime that had the verse, "When God closes a door he opens a window." I still get goose-bumps when I look at it. My son and daughter-in-law had finished signing the paperwork for the new school on the day the gift was given to me. Wow! Was this the plan for me all along? All of my training, being a teacher of children of all preschool ages, being a childcare center director, all of the books and materials that I had purchased over the years. Was it all so when the time came that I was prepared for another challenge?

I believe that this is my purpose in life:

*to assist parents and children in a safe learning environment

*to provide an enriching atmosphere for teachers, with the materials they need

*to give myself to those who need guidance along the way.

My life is fulfilled. Mike and Diane moved close to home, opened their own new business, and gave us a handsome grandson. Our daughter Michelle made tenure at Wake Forest University and my husband Joe has been happily retired for several years. The doors to Jamison Street Preschool are still open, and I look forward each day to the challenges that lay ahead of me. My only goals are to provide the best early education that we can to the young children entrusted in our hands and to provide our parents with any education and guidance that we can.

My perspective on this challenging profession is that it has its laughter and tears. When a new parent becomes comfortable with the setting and a child is excited to learn new material, as we watch all the children grow to their full potential, then we know we are successful in life. No problems can be too big for us!

One cannot ask for anything more in life!!

# ☪ Conclusion ☪

I do not know how to end this book successfully. I have given key information that I feel is necessary for anyone who is thinking about becoming a preschool teacher, an assistant, a caregiver, or who just wants to be involved with their closest childcare center.

Whatever you wish to become can be done. Yes, we are not paid in wages as we should be for the responsibility that we have, but what about today's children or even yesterday's child? Who was there to wipe away a tear when a parent/guardian left that child off at a center? Who was there to ease a child's fears when we changed the time in the fall, and it was dark and mommy or daddy had not arrived yet and to the child, they always come before dark? Who was there when a child had a conflict with another child to help guide them? Who was there to give positive reinforcement to a child who was going through the Terrific Twos? Who was there to ease a parent or guardian's mind when they were worried that they weren't spending enough time with their child because they had to work late? Or who was there to encourage a child who was trying to write his/her name or tie a shoe?

Childcare centers are very important so that children have a safe place to go to daily, a place of understanding and a place with compassionate staff. To maintain this, we must have rules and regulations, as well as a director/owner who hires the best staff possible and helps the staff continue on with a broader education to help today's and tomorrow's treasures – OUR CHILDREN.

Please pass this book on to someone you know who might make a difference in a child's life, but has never thought about working in a childcare center. Please remind people who don't understand what is going on in a childcare center that this book is now available to read. Please stop and talk to a lawmaker about the importance of good, quality care for children and the difference teachers make in a child's life. Please keep all teachers, caregivers, assistants, and any others who work with children in your thoughts and prayers as they strive to help children who will become the leaders of our country in the future.

# ࣸ Index ࣸ

ORGANIZATIONS

Florida Association for Child Care Management (FACCM)
      10060 Amberwood Road, Ste #3
      Fort Myers, FL 33913
      1-800-322-2603
      Info@faccm.org

National Association for the Education of Young Children (NAEYC)
      1834 Connecticut Avenue, N.W.
      Washington, DC    20009-5786
      202-232-8777 or 800-424-2460

National Association for Family Day Care
      725 15th Street, N.W.
      Suite 505
      Washington, DC    20005
      202-347-3356

National Black Child Development Institute
      1463 Rhode Island Avenue, N.W.
      Washington, DC    20005
      202-387-1281

National Childcare Association
      1029 Railroad Street
      Conyers, GA    30207
      404-922-8198 or 800-543-7161

National Head Start Association
      1220 King Street
      Suite 200
      Alexandria, VA    22314
      703-739-0875

Supporting Early Education Develops Success (SEEDS)
10060 Amberwood Road, Ste #3
Fort Myers, FL 33913
1-800-322-2603
Info@faccm.org

Southern Association on Children under Six
P.O. Box 5403 Brady Station
Little Rock, AR    72215-5403
501-663-0353

Zero to Three
2000 14th Street North
Suite 380
Arlington, VA    22201-2500
703-528-4300

RESOURCE BOOKS

ABC School Supply, Inc.
3312 North Berkeley Lake Road
Box 100019
Duluth, GA 30096-9419
1-800-669-4222

*Active Learning Series*
Developed by Frank Porter Graham
Child Development Center
University of North Carolina
Chapel Hill, NC

Creative Resources for Infants and Toddlers
http://www.delmar.com

*Creative Teaching with Puppets*
Gryphon House, Inc.
Early Childhood Books
3706 Otis St.
P.O. Box 275
Mt. Rainier, MD 20712
1-800-638-0928

*Creative Curriculum*
>Teaching Strategies
>P. O. Box 42243
>Washington, DC 20015
>800-637-3652

Discount School Supply
>P.O. Box 60000
>San Francisco, CA 94160-3847
>1-800-627-2829

*Faith Alive – A Curriculum Guide*
>Concordia Publishing House
>3558 S. Jefferson Avenue
>St. Louis, MO 63118-3968

*Fun Leaning-Early Start – A Curriculum Guide*
>PO Box 350187
>Jacksonville, FL    32235-0187
>904-744-8140

Good Year Books
>Department GYB
>1900 East Lake Avenue
>Glenview, IL    60025

*Hand-Shaped Art*
>Good Apple, Inc.
>299 Jefferson Rd.
>P.O. Box 480
>Parsippany, NJ 07054-0480

*High Reach Learning – A Curriculum Guide*
>PO Box 410647
>Charlotte, NC    28241-0647
>1-800-729-9988

*High Scope – A Curriculum Guide*
>600 N. River St.
>Ypsilanti, MI 48198-2898
>http://www.highscope.org

*The Instant Curriculum for Busy Teachers of Young Children*
>Pam Schiller and Joan Rossano
>Gryphon House, Inc.
>3706 Otis Street
>Mt. Rainier, MD    20712

J. L. Hammets Co.
>P.O. Box 859057
>Braintree, MA 02185-9057

Kaplan
>P.O. Box 609
>1310 Lewisville-Clemmons Rd.
>Lewisville, NC 27023-0609

*The Mailbox Magazine*
>P.O. Box 29363
>Greensboro, NC 20712

Montessori
>Check your local phone book or:
>http://www.montessori-namta.org

Oriental Trading Company, Inc.
>1-800-228-2269
>http://www.orientaltrading.com

*Toddlers Together – A Curriculum Guide*
*More Toddlers Together – A Curriculum Guide*
>Gryphon House Inc.
>10726 Tucker St.
>Beltsville, MD 20705

*Totline Theme-a-saurus*
*Totline Nature*
*Totline Nursery Rhyme*
*Totline Story Time*
*Totline Toddler*
>Warren Publishing House, Inc.
>PO Box 2250
>Everett, WA    98203

*Wee Care – A Curriculum Guide*
  Bertie W. Kingore & Glenda M. Higbee
  Good Year

*Wee Learn – A Faith Based Curriculum*
  Church Leadership Department
  127 Ninth Avenue North
  Nashville, TN
  Convention Press


## BOOK CLUBS

Children's Book of the Month Club
  Camp Hill, PA 17012
  1-717-918-1111

Early Childhood Teachers Club
  505 Ridge Avenue
  Hanover, PA 17334

Newbridge
  P.O. Box 5268
  Clifton, NJ 07015-5268
  1-800-729-1463

Scholastic Book Club, Inc.
  P.O. Box 7503
  Jefferson City, MO 65102-7503
  1-800-724-6527
  http://www.scholastic.com

# ཅ About the Author ༄

Peggy Steward has been married to her husband Joe for 42 years. Their family includes son Mike and his wife Diane, grandson Cline, and daughter Michelle.

Peggy has been a teacher of children ages one thru five. Currently she is the Director of Jamison Street Preschool (a family-owned business) in Pensacola, Florida.

Over the past 20 years Peggy has given training to parents and other childcare staff, assisted in design layouts of classrooms and created an atmosphere of positive discipline within her classrooms.

Peggy holds a National Child Development Associate Credential, a State of Florida Administrator Credential, an Owner/Operator's license from Department of Children and Families. She has business school experience, and has served two years on the local board of the National Association for the Education of Young Children.

Peggy has an extreme love of all children, and a history of constant training in child development.

# Acknowledgments

I wish to thank the following people for which this book would not be possible without their support.

My daughter-in-law Diane who took my handwritten and typed notes and transformed the papers into an electronic document.

My children Michelle and Mike who not only supported and encouraged my efforts but were a key part of this book. They gave me advice on business and marketing practices, Michelle assisted in the selection of a printer and the fine-tuning before we went to press.

My friend Rose and her daughter Sharon for the memory graphics.

My sister Kerry, who offered support, encouraged and proofread my earlier efforts.

To Valerie for her computer skills helping my material to be transferred to one place.

To all the children, parents, and staff who have been under my care for all these years. And last to my husband, Joe, who accepted the long hours and all the "stuff" in the garage.

www.ingramcontent.com/pod-product-compliance
Lightning Source LLC
LaVergne TN
LVHW021518080426
835509LV00018B/2557